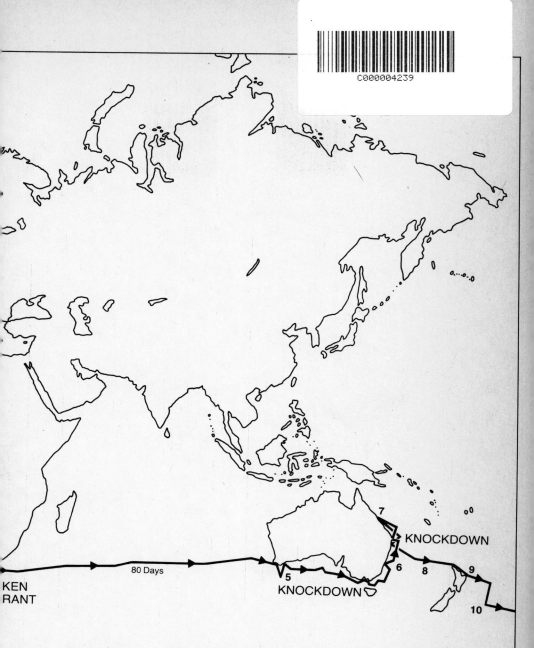

80 Days

KEN
RANT

5
KNOCKDOWN

7
KNOCKDOWN

6

8

9

10

Key

1	Tenerife	**5**	Albany	**9**	Bay of Islands
2	Sal	**6**	Sydney	**10**	Chatham Island
3	St Helena	**7**	Hamilton Island	**11**	Port Stanley
4	Cape Town	**8**	Lord Howe Island	**12**	St Helena
				13	Faial

Not All
Plain Sailing

Not all Plain Sailing

David Sinnett-Jones

WITH
ANN QUEENSBERRY

Foreword by Sir Geraint Evans

Weidenfeld and Nicolson
London

To the doctors and nurses of the National Health
Service who gave me the time to make my voyages.

Published in Great Britain by
George Weidenfeld & Nicolson Limited
91 Clapham High Street
London SW4 7TA

ISBN 0 297 79653 4

Printed in Great Britain by Butler and Tanner Ltd,
Frome and London

Contents

Illustrations

≈≈≈

The photographs in this book come from the author's collection unless otherwise stated.

Foreword

Courage is a virtue I have always admired in those who face adversity.

Having watched my fellow Welshman, David, fight against cancer for the past ten years, seen him teach himself to sail, voyage in a 26 foot boat to South Africa and back via Brazil, build a boat and sail the oceans of the world, I salute his courage.

When he left the small town of Aberaeron, I wondered if, despite his grit and determination, he would survive this adventure. But such a man could cope with the perils of the sea more easily than with the warmth and excitement of the welcome home on his return.

He has a wonderful story to tell and reading his book I feel as though I had sailed the oceans with him.

Geraint Evans

Sir Geraint Evans. CBE

ABERAERON, 1989.

Acknowledgments

~~~~~

I would like to thank the people I love, my friends, helpers, and the HAM radio operators all around the world, without whose help I would not have had the strength to succeed. And without the skill of my sister Ann, who guided my dyslexic self throughout the writing of this book, my task would have been almost impossible. Thank you, Ann cariad.

1

≈≈≈

Building of the Spray

It all started on a pretty average day in the South Atlantic. The sun was high, I had woken from my off-watch morning sleep and picked up an old yachting magazine that had been read and reread many times before on the long voyage. Neville Holloway, crew member on the return leg of my journey from the small Welsh sailing harbour of Aberaeron to see my daughter in Cape Town, was sitting in the sun keeping a lookout for ships, which we rarely ever saw. I showed him an article about the building of a copy of Joshua Slocum's *Spray*. Almost a hundred years ago, in his wooden boat *Spray*, Joshua Slocum had been the first solo circumnavigator. For a long time I had been thinking about building myself a larger boat in steel, something about 40 foot, with a long straight keel for running down the Trade Winds. What I missed most on this voyage was the lack of room and being able to walk around the decks.

Zane II, the boat I was then sailing, was only 26 foot long. A Colvic bilge keeler, she was a good craft that had carried me 20,000 miles in the past three years, but felt cramped when one had been at sea for sixty three days without seeing land, as I had from Recife to Cape Town earlier on this passage. My next voyage was already growing in my mind.

Some months later, after returning home to Bryn Glas, the first task was to persuade my wife Gillian into accepting the idea of my building two steel hulls on the concrete yard outside our now disused cowsheds,

1

and the much easier one of coercing my old friend John Osborne into building one of the hulls for himself while we helped each other in the construction. In this venture I would need a lot of help, as five years earlier in 1978, while farming, I had been diagnosed as having advanced lung cancer, and had to have urgent major surgery to remove one of my lungs and part of the wall of my heart. Luckily a few months earlier I had taken up sub-aqua diving and my doctor had spotted the problem when I went for a medical check-up and X-ray. Twenty years before that, in my motor racing days, I was blinded in the right eye on being thrown through the windscreen of a car, and now at the age of fifty-three was getting a bit stiff in the bones. Some of the worst things that have happened in my life have led the way to some of the most exciting. I would never have started sailing if I hadn't had cancer, nor farming if I had not been in and out of Sir Archibald McIndoe's 'guinea-pig' ward, having seven eye operations and seventy-five stitches in my face. (McIndoe was the pioneer of skin grafting and plastic surgery during the Second World War, treating most of the RAF's severe burn cases, and when I was there the ward still had a very relaxed attitude towards the patients.)

Once John agreed we ordered the plans for the Bruce Roberts's *Spray* and within two months of my return had started the lofting (in the old days the lines of the frames were actually drawn on the floor of a loft). When the first shipment of steel had arrived we welded up John's frames. The strongback, on which to stand the frames, was made out of an old steel-framed harvest trailer. The boards were taken off and, after jacking it up level, legs were welded on and screwed to the concrete, and the strongback was lengthened. The frames were then carried from the workshop to the yard, where they were put in place upside down, spaced and tack-welded to the strongback. The excitement grew as the shape of the finished boat could now be seen, and when the stringers and chine bars were added she took on a personality of her own. Once the plating was started, the marking out and cutting proved to be more of a job than we had first thought, but we were learning all the time and in the ninth month we hired a crane to turn John's 'baby' over. Cutting and making my frames was very quick, as we had made templates of all the pieces and learnt so much on the way that it only took as many weeks to complete my hull as it had taken months to build John's.

A lot of the skills that I had learnt in the past were to be called on.

While I was racing I designed and made parts for formula engines, and welded structures together to make chassis for cars. I was now planning to make a three-bladed variable-pitch propeller. Making drawings of each part to the maximum size that I could turn on my lathe, I then constructed the whole thing in cardboard as I would have done if designing scenery for the theatre.

We were blessed with a mild first winter and as the seasons slid by the decks, pilot houses, and aft-cabins took shape. The day was coming closer when we would have to find a way of transporting John's *Sally Bell* and my *Zane Spray* down to the harbour at Aberaeron. A neighbour, Tegwyn Thomas, who rents my grazing and likes to get involved in such ventures as turning boats over, suggested that Roy Thomas would be just the man for the job. He lives up in the hills behind Tregaron, is a contractor and the owner of a very old four-wheel-drive tractor and low-loading trailer with a gap in the centre of the four back wheels, between which the keel would fit: just what we needed for the job. John and I had worked out a plan. With Acro props welded on to the sides of the hulls we could jack them up high enough to load and unload them on to the trailers, thus saving the further hire of a crane.

Roy arrived with a tractor which had holes in the tyres, headlights hanging off and no road tax! I asked him whether I should inform the police that we would be taking a wide load (12 foot) down lanes of the same width. He suggested that I should send the letter at the last minute so that they would not receive it until the date on which we were doing the moving. This proved to be sound advice.

The first stage was to get my boat out of the yard and as far as the church in the village. All went well until one of the rear wheels of the trailer got caught in the earth bank on the steep sharp bend in my lane. Try as he might, Roy failed to move the trailer any further, so I returned to the house to ring a neighbouring farmer who turned out with his tractor. Both were hitched together and after a lot of wheel-spinning and mud-flying we had to make yet another phone call. With the help of a third tractor she went up the hill to the milk stand. Three cars and a motor-bike leap-frogged ahead to stop and warn the oncoming traffic. Apart from having to lean on a few telegraph poles, the journey went well. A week later we went through the whole operation again. The two boats caused a lot of interest as they stood in the car park awaiting the end of the season when the crane would

3

come to lift the other yachts out of the water and our two in.

The big day arrived. When the crane had finished at the yacht club, it was driven around to the inner harbour, the Pwll Cam, where a large crowd of well-wishers and helpers had assembled. As *Zane Spray* started to lift in the stretching slings, Gillian and I broke a bottle of champagne over her bow and boarded her for the graceful ride above the crowd and down into the dried-out harbour bottom. John's was next, and the two *Sprays* stood side by side. Sally, John's wife, had prepared food and we had brought a five-gallon cask of ale for the helpers. Thus far we felt very proud of our achievement.

The next job was to make the masts. We found some clear, unknotted Douglas fir in a timber yard that was in the hands of the receivers in Glastonbury, and for £350 bought enough wood to build the booms and masts. We converted the cowshed by building level trestles in each of the stalls, having worked out that when finished we would just get the 45-foot masts through the barn doors. Dave Shute, a carpenter, volunteered to help us. He brought his wood-working machine and a router and, with our help, made and dry-fitted the two masts. We then had to glue-assemble them. As it was in the middle of a cold winter spell we made a polythene tunnel and used a fan heater to keep the temperature high enough to allow the glue to set.

During this time I had gone to the Boat Show to meet George Porter. He had shown a lot of interest in my past endeavours and had said that if I ever needed any scrap stainless steel I should contact him at his firm in London. John drove to meet us at the factory. I needed the steel to make two three-bladed variable-pitch propellers, and George had asked for a list of sizes. Instead of taking the pieces out of the scrap bin he started to cut them from a brand new sheet. My heart sank as I knew that $\frac{3}{8}$-inch steel would cost a fortune. By the time we had loaded it all into the van it was nearly down to its wheel arches. I asked George for a box of stainless steel welding rods and then, rather worriedly, how much we owed him. He replied, 'I'm sorry David, you will have to pay for the rods. The stainless steel is free.' John and I drove very happily down the wet M4 to Wales.

Now the machining of the propellers could start. I have only a Myford M7 lathe, so that all the pieces had to be turned up first, then welded together, filled and hand-fitted. It took me two days to balance the propeller but when it was fitted on *Zane Spray*, and revved out of the water, there was no vibration.

The ballast was to be sand and cement and all the scrap steel cut into lengths that would fit into the bays inside the keel. Friends would turn up with their own shovels and help John mix while I filled in the bays and levelled the floors off.

Zane Spray is 36 feet long, with a 12-foot beam and 4-foot draft and a centre cockpit. She is split into three cabins: aft, fore, and pilot house, is cutter-rigged (twin headsails) carrying 1,000 square feet of sail. The auxiliary is a Massey Ferguson 165 tractor engine that I marinized with second-hand parts. The idea of using a Massey was that I thought that wherever I might go in the world, I would be bound to find one in the corner of a field. There is no gearbox but the transmission is through five belts and two-to-one reduction pulleys straight to the propeller shaft. I made a clutch for the large pulley on the prop-shaft so that when released it can freewheel and drive an alternator with the propeller to charge the batteries while sailing. I haven't as yet made the clutch release. Forward, neutral and reverse are found through a control in the cockpit to the variable-pitch propeller.

One Sunday we went to the yacht club and, as the bar closed, rounded up as many hands as we could to help step the masts. The mast was bolted in the tabernacle. The six tallest lads raised it from the aft deck and the rest of them on the quayside heaved on a halyard. Once it was up, John and I worked into the late evening finishing the partly prepared rigging.

We made the water and diesel tanks next and fitted them in place. As we had so far made everything ourselves we thought that we had better make our own sails as well. The mainsail was to be similar to the Hood system, furling behind the mast and loose-footed on the boom. We also made twin furling headsails, a jib and a staysail. My GP, Dr Herbert, let us use a shop he had bought to convert into surgeries for the making of the sails, as the floor was just long and wide enough. We copied the Genoa from *Zane* II, making it a little larger to use as the staysail for the *Sprays*, using the same style of construction for the jib but with a high-cut foot. The main followed, each sail seeming easier than the last. In all we made three sails for each boat, but with no spares I was to take with me a roll of cloth and an electric zig-zag sewing machine.

When I started the carpentry on the cabins, I first constructed a berth in the pilot house that I could sleep in between watches at sea and keep a lookout without going outside. It was already proving useful as I could see the approach of people who would, I knew, keep me talking and stop work on the boat. As Joshua used to put it, 'He would lean on his adze and gam awhile.' The Tourist Board arrange a walk around the points of interest in Aberaeron and they asked for information about my voyage. Many came to watch and chat and I used to hide and work in the fore-cabin out of sight until they had gone. After making the chart table, I ordered the gas cooker, the heads, pumps, basins and timber. The boat was full of sawdust, shavings and confusion but soon the galley was constructed and I could make meals and sleep aboard to save travelling back to Bryn Glas every night.

John had stopped work on his boat six months before I was due to leave, to help me get mine seaworthy. This was quite a sacrifice as he wanted to see *Sally Bell* sailing, but perhaps he knew that once that I'd gone he would get a bit of peace and quiet! With the sails now on we moved *Zane Spray* from her mud berth, around into the main harbour on the top of a spring tide. She was at last almost seaworthy, so John and I plus a friend decided to take her out for a couple of days on her sea trials. We stocked up with food and beer and, when ready, started the engine with the variable-pitch prop in neutral, turned the control and reversed out of the berth, into forward and slowly out of the harbour entrance. I hadn't had time to put a throttle control into the cockpit and asked John to give the engine a few more revs so that I could clear the harbour entrance. Once at sea we stopped the engine and unfurled the staysail in easy stages, and half the main. She picked up speed straight away in the stiff south-west wind. We put out more sail until we had all the 1,000 square feet up and she raced along, throwing spray into the air and lee scuppers in the foaming water. We took turns at the wheel, each one of us hogging it as long as we could. As we trimmed the sails she got up to 7 knots and then 7.5. We were overjoyed with our work, the boat was good, fast and strong. Old Joshua would have been pleased with us! We got to Abersoch in record time but our list of modifications was getting longer. The five-belt transmission drive to the shaft was slipping, so that we would need a new tensioner. I had no self-steering gear and time was getting close to my proposed September start.

One day, Tom Harrison, a stranger to me, turned up on the quay. 'Hey lad,' he shouted in a strong Lancashire accent, 'Would you like Oldham Batteries to sponsor you?' Naturally I agreed, as tractor batteries are very expensive. He promised to get in touch and said that

I would shortly hear from them. Each week he would turn up by the boat and have a long chat, but still I heard nothing. One day he asked me to drive him to Oldham as we had an appointment with the managing director. On the way Tom kept on saying things like, 'We'll have to play our cards right, lad.' I started to worry, wondering if the old boy (only two years older than myself as it happened) had really worked for Oldham's all his life and knew the director as well as he said he did. As we walked into the factory my fears were laid to rest when the receptionist said, 'Good morning, Tom, it's good to see you again. Mr Farrar is in his office and waiting to see you.' Malcolm Farrer welcomed Tom, who told him what my needs were: three charged and two dry batteries, some instruments and all the cable. These were given to me with no strings attached, and even some batteries for John's boat were included.

Eric Williams is a ham radio operator who supported me on my previous voyage by keeping in touch and passing my position on to the yacht club through John. He found me a Yaesue FT707 transceiver with a whip antenna and tuner, and another radio friend made a gift of a G5RV wire antenna.

I had not intended to make the voyage single-handed, and two members of the yacht club asked if they could join me for part of the journey: Vincent Davies, the harbour master at Aberaeron, who wanted to travel with me as far as Tenerife, and Moc Evans who would have stayed on until Cape Town. We had a meeting on the boat, discussed the finance, and talked about the sort of conditions that we could expect on those passages. Although both had been sailing for many more years than I, they had yet to make an ocean crossing. Unfortunately Vince was advised by his doctor not to make the voyage and poor Moc, who had had one nasty brush with cancer, also had to pull out. Time was getting short and I made up my mind that I would start the voyage single-handed.

Money was running low and I had hoped that the sale of *Zane* II would finance the building of the boat, but shortly after I had arrived home the bottom had fallen out of the yacht market. I had been looking for a sponsor since starting the building of the boats, writing to dozens of firms, some of whom showed interest but then backed out.

I met Phill Davies, known locally as Phill Photo, who takes HTV news film and stills for newspapers. As the media usually give me good coverage I thought that I would ask him if HTV might be interested in me sending back news reports on the voyage, to bring in some money. Phill suggested that I should go and see the opera singer, Sir Geraint Evans, who lives in Aberaeron and is on the board of HTV. Sir Geraint was home at the time and answered the door to my knock. We sat in the sun lounge and he asked about the progress of the boats. We talked about sailing and I put my case to him. He listened intently, then said he would be seeing the chairman of HTV at the Eisteddfod and would have a word with him about my voyage. As we stood up to say goodbye, I put out my hand to shake his. He had half turned away and didn't at first see this. When he did he grasped it with his left hand and we strolled to the garden gate hand in hand. As I walked slowly back to the boat I felt as though I was in a dream. I was so excited at what the future might hold and could hardly contain myself. I had to keep reminding myself that I'd heard it all so many times before, and that although people have the best of intentions they don't always do what they say they're going to do.

Sir Geraint was as good as his word. A few days later I had a phone call from Bob Stokes, the director of HTV's adventure documentary programmes, who asked to meet me on board *Zane Spray*. The meeting took place a few days later. He asked a little about my life and then said that he would like to make a one-hour film about the voyage, telling me what the budget would be and asking me how much I would like, but warned me that if I asked for too much he would not get the film to do. I hadn't a clue and so Bob suggested a figure which I accepted. As time was short, he would need to start filming within two weeks to catch all the inevitable last-minute panics in the week before I was to leave. When the contract arrived it was so generously open-ended that if I had changed my mind the next day I wouldn't have had to return the money. Bob had got me more than he had mentioned and at no time put me under any pressure to complete the voyage, realizing how much I wanted to complete the task that I had set myself: to sail around the world via Cape Horn.

With financial problems eased, I could now order the Sailomat self-steering gear. This I had seen on other boats during my first voyage and the owners could never fault them. I needed the best self-steering that I could buy. When sailing solo they are the best crew you will ever get – they neither drink, eat, smoke nor answer you back, their only fault being that they can't share a joke!

The filming started a week before I was due to leave. I had to get used to the crew and being followed everywhere by the camera, Bob asking for each job that I was doing to be done again so that they could get another angle. They gave me a Sony Walkman to make audio tapes on the voyage and a Bolex 16 mm film camera to keep a record for the film. The filming went well, with the added excitement of the fact that I had named the day that I intended to leave. It was a case of the boat being ready but only just. It was still very basic. The more that we could do during this time the less I would have to do at sea.

Jack Harmsworth, the steward of the yacht club, said that we could use the club cash-and-carry card to do the shopping for my stores in Aberystwyth. Followed by the entire film crew, we went on a spending spree. I had learnt a lot on my first voyage: not to waste time by varnishing all the tinned food against rust, nor to work out every meal for each day of the week; just make a list of all the items and then buy as many cases of each as might be necessary for six months, ample to get me to South Africa.

For the past three years, I had watched the world revolving each night on the BBC News, as I had before my first voyage, wondering what the hell I had talked myself into. My sister, Ann Queensberry, drove down from London and helped me sort out stores on the boat. On the morning I was due to leave I woke feeling sick after a restless night's sleep, having dreamed that I had already sailed around the world three times. My son Gawaine and his wife Jackie arrived, and we drove the twelve miles down to the harbour where a crowd was already forming. John rang the coastguard to get the weather forecast. It was bad: force eight to nine from the south-west, right on the nose; my worst fears had come true. The seas were massive at the harbour's entrance and the swell was coming right back, making the boats on their moorings leap into the air, showing their keels. For my first voyage it had been a perfect day. I had left and was over the horizon within hours, but it was not to be so this time.

The highlight of the day was the good-natured way the crowd took the news that I would have to try again tomorrow. Bill Scofield, from the Isle of Man, had come over on the ferry and driven down to see me off. He handed me a cardboard box, saying, 'Stick that on your boat, David. I think it might be useful.' It was a Walker Satellite Navigator. What a good friend! Bob had the film crew ready for my departure; a boat had been hired to follow *Zane Spray*, and a helicopter to do the aerial shots. They managed to do some seascape filming, and I asked Bob if Gillian could go up in the chopper, which for years had been an ambition of hers. We all had drinks in the yacht club and I remember thinking how pleasant it was and that if I had left I would now be on my own.

Another day went by and another gale warning, but on the third day, 17 September 1985, exactly three years to the day from my arrival home in *Zane* II, the weather was right to leave. A large crowd was waiting, the sea was rough and the wind still from the south-west, but I was going. I rang Neil Hughes, the HTV cameraman, to say that today was the day. John, joined by two local fishermen, Lloyd and Danny Thomas, started to get the mooring warps singled up. Gillian called the Llangeitho School so that they could get the school bus to bring them down to see me off, bearing half a dozen homemade mugs. Ready to leave, I got a message asking me to wait for the 'Wales at Six' news team to arrive. The crowd and the excitement was growing and I was impatient to leave. At last the news interview, gifts from the crowd, the Aberaeron school children marching down to the harbour in columns of two, a last kiss from Gillian in front of the cameras, the excitement almost unbearable as the warps and my ties with the warm quay were cast off. I started the engine and motored back out of the berth and then had my first panic. I couldn't get the propeller out of reverse and was heading straight for a friend's yacht while uninsured. I stopped the engine and found that I could now move the control into forward. Restarting, I motored out to sea to the cheering crowds.

2

Stormy Start

At sea now for about two and a half hours. Been through the usual emotions, a few tears in the cockpit and that sort of thing. I had a marvellous send-off. Bloody great. Neil of HTV was filming and said, 'See you in Sydney, Dave.' I'm looking forward to that. There've been a few problems because I've had to learn to sail this on my own in the first few minutes, and have worn myself out. Am feeling shattered so I've set a course going slightly to the north-west, heading for Dublin. It must be the Guinness that's pulling me!

Had a rest for about an hour just to get some steam back. I put up more sail and tacked to head back towards Fishguard. This was my first tack and went quite easily. I was surprised. I turned the wind vane through 90°, swung the wheel over, backed the jib and around she came. I wouldn't like to do it in a confined space.

Having a bit of bother with the Sat. Nav. (Satellite Navigator). It doesn't seem to want to give me a fix that I can rely on; the last was in Llandyissul, which I'm not going to take too seriously. The halyard on the mainsail looks as though it has come adrift, but luckily there are about three turns of the main furled up so it can't fall down. I'm going to have to keep it like that until I get to Tenerife because it's going to be an up-the-mast job to tie it back on. Until then I can't hope to let all the sail out. When I get a nice hot day and it's calm, I

11

might get the binoculars out and have a good look to see exactly what's happened. But for the moment I can't take any chance on that.

I feel grotty this morning. I really didn't want to leave. I was all ready on Sunday. On Monday I was still prepared, but Ann and I used the time to finish off a lot of jobs and tidy the boat up to get her more ready for the sea. *Zane Spray* seems very heavy. I'm surprised how low she is in the water, but in the last few days I must have brought on a couple of tons of food, tools and spares. I hope to get some sleep soon. I have a headache and would rather have done anything than set sail this morning.

I've been mucked around this afternoon rather a lot by Aberporth. Made one tack about fifteen to twenty miles out after leaving Aberaeron, and then a tack back in, heading as far down the coast as I could. The winds had gone light, and suddenly a boat came up and shouted that the range was closed (the Aberporth rocket range). I called range control on the VHF radio, and they told me to either come in close to the shore or head to the north-east which would have put me on the beach at New Quay. I told them that I was single-handed and that they might have warned the coastguard that they had a scheme on. Eventually I came in close, but it was 18.00 hours before they gave me the all clear and I'm now about halfway between Aberporth and Cardigan Island. I've set a new course which is heading me vaguely north-west again and all I can do is go about twenty miles and then tack back, and maybe one day I will get out of Cardigan Bay. It's a nice evening now and porpoise have just started jumping around the boat.

DAY TWO

I haven't had any sleep yet and I'm dead tired. After Aberporth I was left close in to the shore without much wind, so I had to start the engine and motor out a bit. The transmission belts started to slip. I stopped as I thought that they might need adjusting. The wind came up and this morning I was somewhere down by Ramsey Island. I couldn't see it, it was covered in fog.

I've found out why the belts were slipping. The bolt that holds the tensioner to the engine had broken, sheared off. I hope that is not going to be a problem. I've put a new bolt in, tightened it up and adjusted the belts.

The Sat. Nav. is working fine now. I hadn't put in all the zeros. If all else fails, read the instructions – as Lord Nuffield said!

A tanker just passed by, pumping out his tanks in the middle of the Irish Sea, bright yellow stuff. I don't know what it is but it's left a streak from horizon to horizon. I'm going to cross it in a minute. I hope it doesn't stick to my boat.

DAY THREE

To put it mildly, that was a bloody awful night. I haven't spent a night quite like that for a long time. I'm in the middle of the spring tides; very light winds so I couldn't make much headway against the current. I was sailing in the right direction but gradually drifting backwards up the Irish Sea. After half tide it would reverse and take me back again, so I was hoping for a bit of reasonable wind in the right direction. It was right on the nose as usual but good and strong, so I used it to the best of my ability, bombing along for five hours and making good way right up to Tusker Rock on the Irish coast. Then back towards Small's Lighthouse on the Welsh side, and the tide helped me down and out of the Irish Sea.

When I went to tack I found that the mainsail had pulled about three feet of track off the boom. I nearly turned back. I'm not able to sail to windward without getting the main out. I'm restricted already with the halyard off the main and that's stopping her performance. I debated for a long time. I was seasick: the second time in the last twenty-four hours, although I'm taking the pills. I thought I'd better have a go and see what I could do before running back downwind to Fishguard and trying to sort out this God-awful mess. I started the engine, brought her up to the wind and furled all the sails. She's pitching like a bastard. It's really nasty. Choppy, wet, damp, and coldish weather.

Put the main away and lashed down the track with rope and gaffer tape. The HTV boys swore by it. They reckoned that TV studios couldn't survive without it. So gaffer tape it was. Out with the main just far enough to go to windward. I'm not worried about going downwind: I could always put the chute up or twin headsails. I haven't given up yet, not quite. I've got her sailing to windward, and I'm trying to scrape past Small's Lighthouse. The forecast is slightly better but they have been promising all sorts of things. Yesterday it was supposed to go southerly to south-east and it didn't happen. If I could just go west of the Scillies, then I'm on my way.

By a quarter past ten I was over most of my frustration and sickness and had got her going at last. She's now doing 5 knots in quite heavy seas in the traffic separation lanes off Small's. It must be a record, two days to Small's. I started the engine just now to get across the lanes because I was going down a one-way street the wrong way. I'm sure the big ships wouldn't have appreciated meeting me so I put the engine on for about a quarter of an hour, and found a water leak on the shaft. This had happened on *Zane* II. I had to pump out the bilges three times a day, and at the moment I'm doing it daily. I did it yesterday and wondered why I'd had to. I thought we must have forgotten before I left, but in fact it is dripping quite merrily from the shaft. The sealing gland has blown apart but will have to wait until I get to Tenerife. These little things are sent to try us.

DAY FOUR

My position is 51° 00'N 06° 20'W, and I promptly got becalmed. I just sat there wallowing and thought I'd better charge the batteries. I started the engine, ran it for about quarter of an hour and must have had the pitch on the propeller just right because she was doing between 4 and 5 knots when I heard a bang. I switched the engine off and it was the bloody bolt again on the tensioner, so I took it all to pieces. I had to shorten the bush by about half an inch which made the bolt longer and hopefully it will do. It could be that. The bolts I'm using are not exactly high tensile. I'll have to see. The tensioner is like a long bottle-screw which pushes the engine over to tighten the belts. I could put the end of it up against the block with a piece of rubber in between and push the block like that, but it might knock a hole in the side of the engine. I have got my small battery charger, a little Mase generator with a two-stroke engine, and could keep the batteries charged on that for quite a while, so hopefully we'll bomb along. I'm in better spirits. When you haven't slept for two days and the pressure has been on and bits and pieces are falling apart you tend to think, 'My God, what am I doing here?' What a struggle it was to get out of Cardigan Bay!

I haven't eaten much: a little cereal this morning and Irish stew last night with some beans slung in it. I have been seasick far more than on my last voyage, but hope it will settle down in a couple of days.

Concorde has just gone over. I'd forgotten what a noise she makes when everything is still and quiet around. When she goes through the sound barrier, by heck she makes a boom! I was scanning the horizon for the tanker that had just blown up!

The mast is bowing and is tending to bend the deck in front of the tabernacle. An endless, endless list of things to repair. My biggest dread is turning back, bloody failing. If I do I'll have to spend the whole winter repairing the boat and set off again next spring.

I heard the forecast and a gale is heading this way. I hope she holds together. If I can get to Tenerife I can do most of the work there. It means slipping the boat and doing the welding and all the repairs while ashore, but that wouldn't be too bad. It's much easier to work in the sun. I hope I can make it. I feel bloody depressed.

My first gale. I'm in the middle of Fastnet and she's blowing a hooley out there. The tabernacle is creaking right above my head. I'm jammed into the space at the bottom of the steps in the fore-cabin. The mast step or tabernacle is moving and bending the deck head. Another little job. The boat is humming like a dynamo but she's doing much better than the skipper.

DAY FIVE AND MIDDAY

I have a force eight to nine and managed to keep going all night, sailing slowly in the right direction, but it's so bad this morning I've had to lie ahull and have blown back up north again. I've lost about ten miles already. Let's hope to hell it doesn't last too long otherwise I'll be back in Cardigan Bay. That would really defeat me. It would be the end. I could sail home in a day in this. Just straight downwind. This is crazy. Another couple of hundred miles south and I'd be in reasonable weather.

It's still howling away out there but receding very slightly. I had an accident this morning. The boat literally took off from the top of a wave and fell down. They're fair seas not big ocean waves: steep little ones about eight to nine feet high. A gallon of orange squash in a plastic container took off and went into orbit around the fore-cabin, landed and smashed. A gallon of orange squash, concentrated, floating around the floor! I managed to mop it all up.

I had a nasty fright just now. I've had to rely heavily on the Sat.

Nav. because I've only had glimpses of the sun. I've been around once and am now making my second circle in Fastnet. I had a wrong fix on the Sat. Nav. which put me drifting quickly up towards Milford Haven. The only thing I could have done then would be to put a foresail up and run with it back into Cardigan Bay. Luckily it was a false reading. I couldn't understand how I had done that distance, but you just can't tell with a strange boat in these conditions. I don't know how far she is going to get blown along.

I have a tiny triangle of foresail backed and a bit of main to steady the boat. The self-steering is holding her pointing into the seas and she lies ahull like that, sideways on. A bit hairy when you get big 'uns, but she's not moving forward much. She records half a knot and sometimes a knot, but mostly it's fairly low. All I can do is to sit it out. Jesus, Jesus! That was real green stuff. Luckily I had a board in the main hatch. Got some inside but not much. I could see through the windows, through the wave, it was right above the boat.

DAY SIX

Warning of gales. Much better day today, rid of all the storms. Still a bit of a swell up. A few breakers now and again and we're sailing straight out west. I'm only doing about three, three and a half knots and it's probably about force four. I should be going much faster than this. Of course I have brought on a lot of stores, so she is considerably heavier. Maybe I've just got to eat my way through all that weight. All I need is a slightly freer wind. A few degrees either way would make all the difference and I could set a course south-west.

Nothing much happened today, I even got down to washing the dishes. I'm still not eating much, but haven't given up drinking! The odd tin with a few beans slung in, or bread and cheese. Yesterday I had sardines. I think I must catch up on some sleep. I have to put my head down whenever possible because I'm not sleeping enough.

I can't get through to Eric on the ham radio. I can't face putting up the G5RV wire antenna. It would mean getting into wet-weather gear and going on the foredeck, but she's still taking them over the top and I don't feel like getting any wetter than I am already. I found the milk and more orange juice today; quite a job it was, searching around the boat.

What I experienced on my last voyage is happening again. I used

16

to sense someone standing behind me. It was quite a nice feeling and not at all frightening. Sometimes I would turn as if to say, 'Did you see that?' I think most people on their own feel as though there is someone else on board. This has been slightly different. Whenever I wake up I move around very quietly, not wanting to wake the others up. It sounds ridiculous but I've felt Ann on the boat quite a lot too. I've gone to say, 'Did you hear that, Ann?' or 'Where's the milk?'. Odd that.

I have been at sea six days and haven't felt particularly lonely. Too many frustrations and too much to think about. I'm quite happy trolling along, but what I'd like to see is a free wind and this lovely boat doing 6 or 7 knots downwind. It would suit me fine, 150 miles a day plus. I should be able to feel the days getting warmer as I headed south. I'm becalmed about ten miles north-east of the Scilly Isles. I left this time last week. On my last voyage it was only two days' run. This has taken seven.

As the winds were so light, I started the engine and motored to the west, away from the traffic separation lanes by the islands. The bolt in the tensioner was alright, but after twenty minutes there was a screeching noise and I knew that either the belts were slipping or something new was going wrong. It was the small pulley on the engine flywheel. To repair it meant taking all the belts off and removing the pulley and shaft from the flywheel. I found a key and assembled it together with epoxy glue. We hadn't fitted a key at first, as with Fenner Taper Lock pulleys it seemed like using belt and braces. I hope it works alright because it's useful if you need to get in or out of harbour, or even charge the batteries. I can't take the engine out of gear yet as I haven't made a clutch release, and at this point when charging the batteries I'm driving the boat as well. I'm getting frightened of starting the engine in case anything else goes wrong.

Last night I got so depressed. I put up the wire antenna to try to raise Eric as I have been out of touch since Day Two. He must have been listening out for me on the 20-metre band on the hour. I wanted to tell him that I had been thinking of coming back because of all the problems I had yesterday. I was in tears at one point. It's been driving me to despair, not being able to do anything, most of it my own fault on the work side – things that I have built, so I've only myself to blame. John said to me a couple of weeks ago, 'Are you sure you are ready, Dave? Why not put it off for six months and go in the spring?'

He was right and I knew it at the time, but I told him that if I did that I would always find more and more to do. What I should have done was to go on a shakedown cruise around home waters for a few months. I might end up doing that yet! I don't give up easily, but on your own and not too strong things begin to get difficult.

I moved a lot of heavy things about the boat today to try and get her a bit better balanced. She was a bit arse-down, and I humped stuff from one end of the boat to the other. I have to sit down between each load. I've moved a lot and it's easier to get into the aft-cabin.

When the wind comes up again let it be strong so that I can beat into it. I'm not making much headway: about thirty miles south against a south-west wind in the last twenty-four hours. Tacking this morning to the west, the wind absolutely died, just a zenith, zero zero zero on the log. I've 531 miles on it. It was showing 73 when I left home, and what have I covered? Maybe 200 miles, if that. I should be able to get Eric at this distance.

This is crunch time. I've been trying and trying and trying and I'm defeated. I got the pulley done and made a fine job of it. It works very well. I ran the engine for about twenty minutes and smoke started blowing out of the cabin, I could hardly breathe. I knew I must get down there and see what was wrong. I switched the engine off only to see paint burning off the clutch. That's probably been the trouble since the start, the clutch slipping and overheating the belts, which then slip.

It was very hot, but I managed to take it to pieces and tried to think what I could use to pack out the clutch plate. I did some daft things in my motor racing days and got away with them, but not this time. I tried packing it with gaffer tape, ran the engine again, the clutch slipped, overheated and burnt the tape out. I can't think what to do and there's hardly enough wind to fill the sails. She's not moving at all. Perhaps a glass of Scotch and I'll sit this calm out.

I was tired and every muscle and bone in my body ached. After a couple of hours' sleep I got up and, tidying up and checking around the boat, I noticed that the Sat. Nav. was off. I'd seen that before, the voltage was down. I got out the volt-meter and checked that the isolated engine battery was still showing 13 volts. The other two weren't showing a glimmer, and I thought I had run the batteries down dead flat. There was nothing else to do but to get the Mase out and charge them up again, as I couldn't use the main engine. I stood the noise for an hour, standing outside on the deck. It seemed such an intrusion into the peace of the ocean. The fumes kept on wafting into the cabin and I was getting quite happy on them. An hour was not enough but it would get me through the night. What the hell, I thought, I'll drill that hole in the clutch while I have the Mase on. John and I had talked about doing this in an emergency, drilling a hole straight through the lot – clutch, plate and flywheel. That would stop it slipping. I got the tools out and drilled the hole and knocked in the quarter-inch stainless steel pin and found I'd worked half the bloody night. It's about one o'clock now, and I have just had a nice corned beef sarnie and a couple of large Scotches to celebrate. We'll have to see if it will be good enough in the clarity of dawn. Right now I'm absolutely shattered. I had terible cramp in my chest today. It comes when I overdo things and the pain is like a knife.

I slept all night and woke to rain this morning. It's still dark and the wind was coming from the south-south-east. This is decision time: north or south, and – good news – it's south. I'm heading for Tenerife. Even with the existing problems I think I can cope. However, two of the batteries were absolutely flat this morning. Not the engine one, the two auxiliaries for the Sat. Nav., radios and lights. I carry lights at night because there's quite a bit of shipping about.

Maybe the Sailomat rudder isn't big enough. There is a larger size and I'll have to see if I can get one somewhere. Everything must be just right for it to work, the right balance between the sails and helm, so that she'll take over.

It's thick fog and I suppose I can see about a 50-foot radius round the boat. A bright sky, no blue or anything but it's lighter, brighter above. Not particularly cold, but I feel I can hear foghorns that aren't actually there. A funny little murmur on the boat, that dynamo sound. I don't like fog, although I don't see why it should be any worse than anything else. Hopefully ships would be more watchful, have their radar on and be keeping a good eye out for other vessels, though not necessarily small boats. With any luck, having a steel hull will make a good reflection. We'll find out. Heading south might be slow, but at least we're heading south and west.

It's surprising how much west you need in a course when you leave the British Isles. In *The Ocean Passages of the World*, a book written for the old square-rigged ships with sailing directions on how to sail the trade routes, they tell you to make as much west as you can, because you don't want to get inbayed in Biscay. I thought it was a lovely expression, 'inbayed in Biscay'. You can sail out of Cardigan Bay and go due west for maybe four or five days. It's surprising how far Spain and Portugal stick out at the other end of Biscay. I like to be about two or three hundred miles off Portugal. Africa starts sticking out more and more and you need quite a lot of west in your course. I like to get a bit of sea room to start off with. I'm doing well at present. I've left the Scillies behind.

DAY NINE

I got up at about 12.30 a.m. and she was heading in the wrong direction. The wind had nearly faded away and I put her on a fairly easy course so that she wouldn't gybe again, and went back to bed. By about six o'clock we were creaming along, south-west and a fairly choppy sea from the flat we had last night. She'd taken care of herself beautifully, picked up and gone as she should with the wind.

I've had another look at the oil leak on the engine. The oil's so clean on the dipstick, it's difficult to tell where the level is. I think it's over-filled. I don't know how we could have done that, but it looks as though there's twice as much oil as there should be. It's difficult at sea because the oil doesn't settle, it's thrown around inside the engine.

DAY TEN

I want to get some of the weight out of the aft-cabin and more on the port side. I managed to get to the onions and spuds, but unfortunately I had taped the plastic bags up and the onions and carrots are sweating like mad. I opened all the bags and let them breathe. When we get some sun I'll be able to dry them off and they should keep a bit. I don't know when I'm going to eat all this stuff: there are stacks of apples which I rarely eat. Never mind. If I don't have them, Davy Jones will. It's taken me a long time but is a little clearer now that I've put some stuff up in the bow. I had an empty locker which I've filled with beer and milk.

It will be nice when I get a bit of sun because I haven't cleaned the boat at all inside. I'm just carrying dirt in from the cockpit. I must give it a good sweep and a wash.

The winds are still very light; I'm doing only 2 knots. It came up for a bit and I did 4 but not for long. I need to see this boat sail because at the moment I tend to blame her rather than me and the wind. I'm just wallowing along at 2 knots but she can pick up her heels and go if she gets the wind; I only need the bloody wind....

Shortly after all my moaning the wind came up at about force four, occasional force five from the east, or south-east, somewhere around that direction. I had got a free wind and could sail almost any course that I wanted. I stuck to south-west, and within half an hour I was up to 6 knots and had to take in some of the staysail to protect the mast because of the problem with the lower shrouds. I adjusted the sails and got her back to 4.5, then 5 knots. The wind increased and went around more to the east so I had to free her off. This was something that I haven't had to do since I left home; even when we went to Abersoch we were running hard on the wind most of the time. It took me quite a time to get her sorted out as she kept on wanting to sail up to the wind. I eventually got it and she has been sailing like this ever since. It's grey, damp and overcast, but the sea state is not bad at all, just the usual force four and no large swells.

I have a stowaway. A pigeon landed in the cockpit last night. I went to pick up a strange, dark object and caught hold of something warm. I gave it some toast but it didn't seem interested. It's a racing pigeon and looks sorry for itself and pretty tired. Maybe it will stay for a bit or even do a circumnavigation.

It was a little warmer last night which is good, as after ten days I'm still in the same damp clothes that I left in. It's a good job I'm on my own!

Had to get out of the way of a fishing boat last night and it seemed to take hours. You are never quite sure what's in your path when asleep. I still wake up with crowds of people on the boat and am disappointed when I find no one there. I think it's the worst time: waking up and realizing there's nobody there. But the wind is here, so ride on!

DAY ELEVEN

I've been loading the HTV camera, a Bolex 16 mm. I thought that I had better do so before I forget how to do it. It didn't go badly, but the film wouldn't follow around the tracks and I had to cut the lead twice. I eventually got it behind the slider in front of the lens. I will take some

21

film of 'Pidgey' and the sea, with the Sailomat working, to get used to holding the camera still.

I've got whales within twenty feet of the boat now! Another one came up and dived. He's enormous. Probably about twice the length of the boat. I heard a big bang when one of them went under the keel. It looks as if they are going to hang around for a bit, this is great! I think I have taken some of the worst film ever; I tried to balance on the side of the boat but they don't stay on the surface for more than a few seconds. Another one is blowing. I can see his fins just sliding underneath the water. I hope they don't get too playful. He is right beside the boat, I'm hanging on like mad here! I've never seen them so far north. Something hit the side of the boat then. I hope some of this film comes out. It was a bit precarious: I couldn't see the first shot as I couldn't get my good eye in the eyepiece to see what was happening. I might not get another chance like this.

I had the most extraordinary experience last night. I'm not setting the alarm now: I just sleep and when I wake have a lookout and maybe something to eat, sit there or go back to bed again. I'm sleeping when I want to and staying on watch when I feel like it. But last night one of my imaginary crew awoke me. I had a lookout and saw a red light on the horizon straight ahead. I decided to keep watch for a bit. As we got closer I could see a white light which didn't seem to be moving. I was still heading straight for it. I thought that it must be another yacht, probably sailing up towards me. I shone my torch at it then took the self-steering out of gear and changed course as I was on a collision course. I sailed 200 yards astern of an old wooden fishing boat that was lying ahull with a steadying missen sail. The crew no doubt were all asleep.

Pidgey hasn't eaten anything yet, I don't know what I'm going to do with him. I put him out in the cockpit today as he was beginning to smell. He perked up a bit and drank some fresh water. He was pecking at the salt water in the cockpit and then spitting it out. Perhaps he was trying to tell me something. I tried to interest him in some toast, bacon fat, rind and cereal but he wouldn't touch it. If he lives long enough I might try and shoo him off as I go past Madeira.

This is the thirteenth day and I've just spoken to a ship, the *Scamper Universal*, out of Dover for Mexico, a refrigerated ship going to pick up oranges. I can just see her over the waves; had a chat with a nice Scottish accent and told him about my voyage. He's going to report my position to Lloyd's of London and give them all the news. If he can get the message through it would be terrific. He said that he had been thinking he wouldn't like to be out in a small boat in this weather, and turned around to spot me out there. I said it was sometimes worse on a large ship than a small boat. When I mentioned Pidgey he told me they were often visited by them: they arrive clapped out, disorientated, won't eat and just die in the end. I'm prepared for the worst.

The wind has come up during the day and it's blowing a hooley out there. I'm getting tired and so is Pidgey. I keep going outside to reduce sail and am down to a 3-foot triangle of staysail with not much main out. She is still going along at 3 knots and the seas are mountainous, to put it mildly. The forecast for this area is force five to six. I wish those weather men were here. I'm not far down in Finisterre, as I'm heading west and away from it. I will be in the Azores soon if I'm not careful, but there is nothing I can do about it, just sit this one out. Pidgey is standing half in the engine room. He keeps on getting out of his box, and is looking very sorry for himself. I probably look about the same. I'm frightened, as I usually am in this sort of situation. I'm just looking for that bright bit on the horizon. It's got to come soon.

DAY THIRTEEN

Eleven o'clock at night. Still taking one hell of a beating, hardly any sail up and still doing 2.5 knots to the west. My bunk got soaked when a wave came over the top and through the main hatch. The wind is screaming out there. I've had this too long, too long and another bloody howler. I'm fighting my way down, scratching. I thought I'd be in hot sunshine by now. Oh, that would be good! I'm so tired, so tired.

DAY FOURTEEN: 30 SEPTEMBER 1985

Still in a gale. Spent last night sailing west very slowly, with hardly any sail up. When I got up the batteries were dead flat so I had to start the engine. I turned to the south-east and motor-sailed for two hours. I could go no faster than 1 knot, as even at that speed the hull was crashing into the steep waves. There was a lull earlier but it didn't last long. Everything's wet now except the film camera and the tape recorder. I've taken some seas in as I have been getting in and out of the main hatch. A nasty sea, probably worse than some of the big ocean stuff I had before, down in the South Atlantic where usually you are going with the storms. I'm trying to go straight into the teeth of this, but can't do it, and am just going up and down trying to hold station.

Time now 15.30 hours. I tried the radio, no luck; however, the gale has abated, and I'm now sailing south. Unfortunately Pidgey decided to take a walk around the cabin. I chased and caught him, picked him up and was going to put him out in the cockpit where I usually launch him and he flies to the aft deck. This time he landed, skidded, took off and flew over the rails. I stood in the cockpit watching him go down, as I knew that there was no way I could pick him up. I feel so sorry. I didn't like the little bugger shitting all over the place, but I certainly didn't want to do that to him.

When I went to unfurl the mainsail, I forgot what I was doing and let it all out, the bloody thing slid down the groove. So now I have the most diabolical main ever seen, hanging like an empty flour sack!

AN HOUR LATER

The mainsail is in the aft-cabin. I have to think of a method of getting it back up without going up the mast to fix the halyard. I could pull it up with the topping lift (a halyard for lifting the boom), but would have no way of reefing it. It's a large sail if I were to get caught out. I could put a downhaul on the end of the topping lift, tie the end of the halyard on to the mainsail, pass the other end through the eye of the topping lift and pull it up so that the eye is at the height the head of the sail should be, hoist the sail with the halyard and start furling the main, trapping the halyard as I go and pull down the topping lift with the downhaul. What could be simpler? But should I do it now, tomorrow, or wait until I'm becalmed?

My great plan didn't work and I'm right up the creek without a bloody paddle! I just don't know what to do; I'm right at the end of my tether. I'm a hell of a long way from anywhere. I can't think. The only thing to do is turn around and go home. Oh what a cock-up! The topping lift went round the mast as the boat rolled, through the spreaders, and caught on one of the claw rings so that I couldn't get it free. After all that effort the mainsail is again in the aft-cabin. I feel so inadequate. If I were fit I could pull myself up in a bosun's chair and do the job in no time.

A tanker has just gone past. I didn't call him on the VHF, as I'm sure I would have made it a PAN call. That's an emergency without danger to life. They would have helped me, but I couldn't do it. It's my own fault that I'm here. Somehow I must get myself out of this shit. It would have been too easy to call that ship.

DAY FIFTEEN

I feel very weak and tired. All I want to do is sleep and it's hard to think. I have stopped using the water out of the main tank as it has a peculiar aftertaste. After the tanks were galvanized there was a sort of dust in the bottom. I tried to wash it out but the water is still cloudy and must have been stirred up by the gales. I will use the water out of the plastic containers and see if that makes any difference to the way that I feel: at present like a wet sponge.

DAY SIXTEEN

A fairly rough night. Force eight now and I've just been to reef some more, to find that the jib has a tear near the top. I furled it away without tearing it any more. It's getting bloody desperate now, a bit out of hand. I don't know if I'll ever see land again.

There are so many repairs to do that if I ever reach Tenerife I will surely be there for six months. I suppose my fortunes could change. I could get a force four to force five from the north-east and steady for about two weeks and get the cruising chute up. Then I could take the torn sail down and repair it and get the stays moved back to take the bend out of the mast. I might be able to sail then!

It's half past eight and pretty dark. I am having a fantastic blow now, and every time there is a lull my heart lifts. Then the noise comes back and I slip into lower depths of despair. Christopher Rudd from the Jubilee Sailing Trust for disabled sailors, who crewed on my previous voyage, gave me a balaclava helmet before I left which he had lent me in a force twelve storm we sat out together 250 miles off Cape Town. He said, 'It helped you through the last bad one David, let's hope it will help again.' So I'm sitting here with it on. It's quite warm and I don't need it except for comfort. Three days of continuous bloody storms, not just gales. The seas have been mountainous and foam is flying everywhere. I feel so small out here on my own. Absolute nothingness. Nothing.

3 OCTOBER 1985

It's pounding away out there. Massive big seas, a clear blue sky with a nasty cloudy circle around the horizon and the wind is screaming. The waves are twenty-five feet high and breaking at the top, everything's froth and foam. A beautiful colour if you were watching it on a bit of film, but not out here. The best course that I can make is east; I'm pointing south but getting pushed east, which will take me into the Bay of Biscay. I can survive for another two days like this without getting into trouble with land. But if this continues tomorrow I will have to turn north and west and sit it out. I can't face anything at the moment. I can only sit here and try to keep myself together.

The storm seems to be abating. I ran without light until one o'clock last night and switched off the instruments, put the navigation lights on and went to sleep. I try to save as much energy as possible and use the Sat. Nav. only once a day to find out where I am. I used to have it on all the time in order to know how close to land I was.

I connected the aerial of the small radio to the VHF antenna and have a much stronger signal now. I have started to lose the BBC and forecasts are difficult to receive.

DAY NINETEEN

This morning I was determined to get the mainsail up, first freeing the topping lift by pulling a weighted bucket up on the end of it, waiting until the motion swung it through the spreaders, unhooking it and taking it down before it got caught again. My plan worked this time. Not a good job: it's slack at the top. In fact it looks bloody awful, but it's better than no main at all.

The job took me four hours and I have really overdone it. I feel shattered, my heart is fluttering as it does when I do too much. Before resting I spotted a Dutch ship, the *Brage*. I called them on the VHF and asked them to report my position to Lloyd's, but as I was talking the batteries started to go flat and I had to start the engine. After this I tightened the alternator belt with a piece of wood jammed behind it

26

and tied it down. She ran like that for half an hour and then the belt broke. I will have to make the spacer very soon as it's still too rough to use the Mase outside and there is no other way to charge the batteries. I must get some solar cells.

The wind has come up again, it's force six now and right on the nose, sending me straight towards Cape Finisterre. I tried tacking earlier to see what course I could make, but the best was just north of west which doesn't help. I still don't know whether or not to turn and make for home. With these gales up my arse I'd be there in a week.

Have only enough paraffin for another four to five nights. I like to keep a hurricane lamp burning at night in the pilot house, so that when I wake I know where I am. It makes it easier for my eyes to adjust to the light. I'm still feeling weak, can't do very much and get out of breath quickly. I tried to eat an omelette with corned beef in it this morning, which was disgusting.

The Sailomat has been working beautifully, going to windward and on a broad reach. I tried to set her downwind this morning as I had made up my mind to sail home, but she wouldn't have it at all. It's a bit worrying as most of trade-wind sailing is downwind. It could be that I haven't got the sails balanced. I've had it, mentally and physically. I'm so ashamed. I have to try and make up my mind. I feel faint all the time. It's very difficult to concentrate, to make rational decisions. God, I wish I knew what to do. I'm really desperate. I'm not like this normally, this is a totally new experience. I can usually cope, but it has been so long, and my strength and resistance are down.

It's four o'clock in the morning. The wind died and torrential rain started to fall, it died and left me in a hell of a sea, the waves are crashing into the side of the boat and going right over the top. It's quite horrific the way some of them hit the hull. There is no wind to hold the boat steady and everything in the cabin gets thrown around.

I got stuck into some work, as whatever happens I must be able to charge the batteries. I made two new arms for the alternator out of Tufnel: eight inches long with holes in both ends, bolted on between the bracket on the engine and the alternator. The top adjuster I lengthened similarly with a piece of metal. I tensioned the new longer belt and found that the wires (that go to the alternator) were too close. As I taped them out of the way, all four came off the relay. My first attempt didn't work, there was a lot of smoke, and I thought I'd blown everything up. On the last attempt I started the engine and it bloody well worked, and I don't mind whether it's under or overcharging, it's putting in 30 amps at the moment!

The wind has come back; it always does when it's dark and you can't see what you are doing, but at least it's here and I'm doing 0.3 knots and heading to the west. It's still raining and I'm soaking wet. I put on the top half of my Henry Lloyds (heavy weather clothes) while working outside, and got my jeans soaked. I'll have to leave them on to steam themselves dry overnight. It's a bit uncomfortable but the only way I can do it. Now that I have some power in the batteries I'm going to have a good night's sleep, and see what the Lord brings in the morning.

DAY TWENTY

The wind has gone into the west and I'm sailing at 4 knots to the south-west, what could be better? I put out the Red Ensign. It was time I did that. My prayers have been answered. I am on my way!

3

Plain Sailing

DAY TWENTY-ONE

I ran the engine this morning and motored a few miles as I was almost becalmed. The wind is coming up again. On a good course and making 3 knots. There is a fishing boat about half a mile behind me, Spanish or Portuguese. I'm standing in the cockpit waiting to see if he will come over and say hello. No. He is too busy fishing. My position is 42° 42′N 11° 15′W. I've only to get to 28°N to Los Cristianos, and at sixty miles to the degree, not too bad.

DAY TWENTY-THREE

Sailed nicely all night but the wind has gone a bit light. I've had a hell of a job to get her to sail a good course. She wants only to go up to the wind and sail to the north-west. I noticed that the stop cord on the self-steering wind vane wasn't letting the vane go over to the 30° recommended, so I lengthened the cord and now it's much better, but noticed that there is some play in the rod that goes from the vane to the mechanism inside the Sailomat. One day I must lash the ladder to the aft-rail and go down to see if I can adjust it.

Had some ham, pickle, cheese and biscuits for lunch and the last of my box of wine. There are two bottles of John's elderberry wine stowed away in the cubby hole. Quite powerful stuff. It can lift off your

29

cranium. I think I'm getting a bit short of booze, which is worrying. I did consume rather a lot in the first three weeks, but it was a rather nerve-racking time. Yes, I did knock it back a bit. I wonder if there is any lurking in one of the lockers? I must have a massive search. On my last voyage I searched the whole boat in vain!

A lot of fishing boats about last night. I was crossing a bank 490 metres deep and a boat crossed my bow only 400 yards ahead. Nothing dangerous, but if I had been asleep and he hadn't seen me, well you never know. In the end you get so tired you have to trust in God and go to sleep.

My position at midday was 41° 40'N 12° 42'W: that's a fair little jump. Not much sail up. A bit of the torn jib and the main comes only halfway along the boom, enough to show the HTV sign. I should be in Trafalgar tomorrow. It's only forty miles down the road.

10 OCTOBER 1985

The best day so far, lovely sunshine this morning. The boat had been struggling all night to keep going in very light winds, the sails had been slatting and banging and she was heading on a south-east course. I tried several times to get her on a better heading but the wind was too light. Suddenly the wind got stronger and I'm up to 3 knots. The large swells have gone down as well. Each time we went down in a trough the sails slatted, as they were shaded from the wind.

At last, at last, I've had a good QSO (contact) with Eric. I switched on half an hour early and heard him very faintly. The first time I got most of my position over, then we tried another frequency and couldn't get through, so I waited and he came through loud and clear. He gave me all the news. He had seen Gillian yesterday and all was well. That's great. They all know that I'm safe and well and have my position.

I tried a music tape on the Sony Walkman. I hadn't realized that my tapes were recorded in stereo. With the earphones on I'm in a different world.

DAY TWENTY-FIVE

The wind is very light from the south-east – a great direction, doing 2 knots on the right course. I got up at five to save power by switching off the navigation lights. By sunrise it was so quiet that I went on the foredeck and took the jib down. Not as bad as I had thought. A two-foot seam and eight foot of edging has come unstitched. I opened the forehatch and pushed the top part of the sail down on to the fore-cabin table; I got out the sewing machine, set it up and started the Mase. The machine wouldn't sew. I had lent it to somebody just before I'd left, and it was dropping stitches. After a few test pieces I got it right and rattled through the repair. The sail back on deck, I hoisted it up and now have twin headsails again. Great. That's one job off the list.

I still had the generator out in the cockpit, and as it was pretty calm I thought I should drill the holes for the shackles on the side decks. I made a half-inch hole through the steel plate behind the next frame aft. When I had done both sides I fitted the shackles on and cleaned up the filings. Feeling very happy with my day's work, I went to have a rest.

Eric asked me on the radio if I would record a speech for the Aberaeron Yacht Club dinner, and so that is what I've done.

Did some filming today. I put the camera on its swivel clamp, set it while I did some work around the mast, and shot some footage of the Mase in action.

Had a good night's sleep. I've certainly come to terms with sleeping. On my last voyage I used to get up on the hour, every hour, to have a lookout, check the sails and write a bit in the log, but a ship coming over the horizon could be here in fifteen minutes. Now when I sleep I look out only when I wake up. I try to stay up in the evening and keep watch without lights to save battery power.

I missed the last forecast, but I don't think that I would have been able to hear it. The time before it was getting very faint. I'm nearly at the bottom of Trafalgar now, with only 460 miles to Tenerife – not too far.

Today I fitted the throttle lever in the cockpit. Richard Moffatt, a friend from Wales, bought it at a junk stall at the Southampton Boat Show and gave it to me before I left: a big brass lever which looks good.

DAY TWENTY-NINE: 16 OCTOBER 1985

The wind is blowing at force four and it's still on the quarter. I'm making fine progress. In the last two days I have covered 200 miles, including the time that I was becalmed. Not bad at all.

Had a good contact with Eric and got over a message about parts that need replacing. They can be sent with Captain Dai Evans, who is coming out to Tenerife in late October. I will send a list. I asked if they can get a large rudder for the Sailomat sent out to me. Apparently John is finding out what the stuff is in the bottom of the water tanks. He sent a sample to the people who galvanized them and they think that it is some sort of salt.

I've spotted a bit of paper. I think it might be an egg box. Once I saw a neon tube in the middle of the Atlantic, two thousand miles from anywhere, going over the cresting waves. A big event like that can occupy one's mind for days.

It's warm in the sun, but a cool breeze from the north-east. I sunbathe naked in the morning for an hour, but when I'm in the cabin I need a sweatshirt as the wind coming off the mainsail and through the hatch keeps the cabin quite cool.

DAY THIRTY: 17 OCTOBER 1985

I got up early this morning, took the headlining down in the pilot house and ran the wires through for the cabin lights. Spotted a ship and tried to get through on the VHF but my auxiliary batteries were too low and he couldn't hear. Shortly after that I saw a yacht sailing very slowly towards me. I switched on the radio again, put on the engine battery, then gave him a call. It was an Italian boat. They were five days out from the Mediterranean, their first Atlantic experience. The skipper asked if I could help them as they had flat batteries, could not start the engine, and had been unable to use navigation lights for three days. As they had not enough power to work the water pump, they were having to syphon water out of their tanks. There were two crew: a very tall, fit-looking German and an American girl. I told the skipper, Mario, that they could borrow my generator to charge their batteries. Bert, the German, came over on a sail-board to collect the Mase and my inflatable dinghy to take it back in. We sailed alongside each other for the next three hours and I could hear the buzz of my little generator in the cockpit. If they had sailed off with it, I wouldn't have been able to start my engine either, as my batteries are flat. They returned the Mase with a bottle of wine and a loaf of bread. They are also heading for Los Cristianos and I hope to meet them there. It's rare to meet another yacht at sea, let alone stop and talk. After thirty days

32

alone to talk to someone was terrific!

When they had disappeared motoring over the horizon, the quietness and loneliness hit me again. It wasn't long before *Zane Spray* was alive to the sound of the Mase recharging the batteries and the Treorchy Male Voice Choir. It brought tears to my eyes but drowned out the Mase.

DAY THIRTY-ONE

Haven't got a position yet this morning but I don't think that I have moved very far. You can hear the silence, it's just broken by the occasional slatting of the sails and the noise of the water going up and down in the cockpit drains. The water is like glass, with the sun beating down on the sea. It's a glass desert. I slept well last night. There were a lot of fishing boats around and each time I woke there seemed to be one close.

I did some motoring, as the batteries needed charging again, and noticed a yacht following me. It stayed behind me for fifteen minutes and then stopped. I wondered if it could be the Italian boat again and motored back to see. It was a French yacht, with a man, woman and a child aboard. They didn't have much English but asked if I was going to Madeira and if all was well with me. I wished them *bon voyage* and we parted company.

Before trying the radio I decided to run the engine, and swapped from the port to the starboard diesel tank, but after ten minutes the engine stopped. I thought that I had sucked up some air and had an airlock. Switching back to the port tank I started to bleed the system. It seemed to take forever but after a lot of cranking and wasted battery power she finally sprang to life. As there was no wind and it was very hot in the boat, I carried on motoring. A short time later I went to see if it was still charging, to find that a pipe on the injector pump was broken and there was a hell of a mess, diesel everywhere. I stopped the engine and replaced the pipe with hard nylon tubing, and went through the process of bleeding the system again. The batteries were still flat, so I ran the engine and the Mase at the same time. The noise was unbearable but it had to be done.

The wind came back an hour ago, this time from the north-west, as far as I can tell. It's not really strong enough yet, but I'm doing half a knot on the right course and she is picking up. I need a bit of wind through the boat to cool it down, there's still so much heat coming off the engine, though it's been off for a few hours now.

There was a Russian ship on a collision course with me for a time. He was on the same heading from the time I spotted him coming over the horizon. I tried to get him on the radio but the only reply was a lot of clicks, which can be made by pressing the on/off button on the mike. I think he saw me. I was getting worried as he got closer, but at the last minute he turned and went to my stern.

DAY THIRTY-TWO

The wind dropped after coming up a little this morning. I thought that I was away but the little wind there is, is from the north-west. There are mares' tails in the sky so maybe things will improve later.

Had a good QSO with Eric. He was in his car in a traffic jam in Aberaeron, and I talked to him all the way to the yacht club. The yachts were being lifted out of the water by crane, so a lot of my friends were down by the harbour. Eric told me that Ann was in Sweden doing a film and that Gillian had started an Open University course in Tregaron.

I was ill last night, having found a packet of egg noodles and Parmesan cheese that Ann had left on the boat, with a note wishing me a very happy supper! There were cooking instructions in German: all I could understand was fifteen minutes and not whether to boil or fry them. I settled for boiling and sprinkled the cheese on the top. I enjoyed it and sat out in the evening cool with a coffee and another Scotch. I was still alright when I went to sleep but one hour later I was violently sick and again twice in the night. I lost my breath and was gasping in the dark, very weak, alone, and cold. This morning I'm like a piece of wet brown paper. I hope I feel in a better skin later.

The sun is just going down. I try to keep watch without lights, using the paraffin lamp. It's not easy to stay awake sitting in the dark. The last few days I've only managed until about ten o'clock at night before weakening and going to bed.

I'm rather depressed about my progress. It's taken three days to do one decent day's run. I felt a bit worn down by sickness, but it seems to be going and I've eaten toast and Marmite today. It's taken thirty-two days to get this far, that's terribly slow. Fish are jumping clear of the still water and I'm nearly becalmed again. Perhaps they are trying to get oxygen as the sea is flat. When she is rolling and seems not to be moving, if you throw an empty beer can over, in about ten minutes it's a boat's length away. That's a good sign.

DAY THIRTY-THREE

No wind today and not much all night. Only enough to make ten miles with a half-knot current underneath helping me. A ship has just gone by, only a few hundred yards ahead. A real old rust bucket, people walking on the deck, and a lot of banging and crashing going on. I tried to contact them on the radio but no reply. I think they are Arabs.

Saw another ship, the *Maersk Harrier* and had a long chat on the VHF to them. They left Milford Haven for Ascension Island to top up a company tanker, with a cargo of kerosene. They told me that the trip only takes them twelve days and they might see me on the way back if I'm still becalmed. Wishing me luck they went on their way.

I did some filming in the cockpit of me doing the washing, ready for shore leave. I had been moping as it is hot, sultry and calm. Tomorrow I shall cut my beard.

Sometime I'm going to take the thermostat out of the engine to see if I can get it to run cooler, as it is very hot outside, in the middle eighties. Perhaps I'll put a pipe over where the dipstick goes in, as when I run the engine for more than an hour the oil starts to fry on the side of the block and the fumes come bellowing out of the engine room.

No contact with Eric today. Sunday is a bad day as everyone is at home and on the air. One guy was painting his ceiling and talking to Canada at the same time. He carried on for half an hour describing what part of the ceiling he had got to. I broke in to give Eric a call, and the ceiling man came back with, 'The frequency is in use, old man.' I listened for Eric until the ceiling was completed.

DAY THIRTY-FOUR

I'm sailing, I'm sailing! She is moving again and the sea has lost its shine. The wind has come back, just steady, but it's come back, it's crept up on me, the sails are full, more or less. Oh, I hope it lasts! I have been becalmed for four days, the last two moving forward only on the engine.

LATER

The bloody wind stopped, it only lasted an hour. I went forward about three miles in that time, then it stopped. Occasionally there's a little breeze and we go forward a few yards and then stop. I'm still becalmed. Only eight-five miles north of the Salvage Islands a hundred miles north of Tenerife. It's hard to take.

DAY THIRTY-FIVE: 22 OCTOBER 1985

Have a bad headache and a pain around my gall bladder from when I was sick. Very depressed. The wind didn't come back. I haven't moved all night – my fifth day of being becalmed– and tomorrow Dai Evans flies to Tenerife and I still have nearly 200 miles to go.

There are lots of tortoises around the boat – no, not tortoises, they are turtles. And two birds. One looks like a sparrow, the other has a long tail, a dipper or something, I'm not sure. They seem to be hitching a lift and it's nice to have their company. They are having a bit of a battle: the one with the long tail is having a go at the sparrow. They don't like each other very much.

The wind has come back. I'm not getting excited because I'm still doing only half a knot. It's very light and patchy and this is what happened yesterday but I'm thankful to have a bit of wind.

I got down to fitting a pipe from the engine breather and put the other end into the manifold air intake so that it sucks all the fumes from the engine and out with exhaust. For the first time for ages there were no fumes in the cabin and my one lung could breathe again.

I'm only about thirty miles north of the Salvage Grande, the largest of the islands. It's very hot and airless and if it is like this when I pass them I might anchor, have a swim, and sit in the sun on the beach. However, if I have any wind I must press on.

One of the two birds has taken off and headed for land; the other made a nest in my clothes and wouldn't eat or drink. He died so I put him over the side. Life seems so fragile out here.

36

DAY THIRTY-SEVEN

Land ho! Land ho! I've just spotted a lump on the ocean. It's the first land since Ireland thirty-six days ago. It's a bloody pimple on the horizon, just a bloody pimple. Had a hell of a night, the wind came up from the north-west. I was doing nicely, about 1.5 knots, when it started to pour with rain. I got her back on course, stayed with her for half an hour and the wind dropped and left me in a lopping sea. Again the wind came up, but this time from the east. It has settled now, the rain stopped with daylight, and there they are on my starboard bow: the islands.

TWO DAYS LATER

I was surprised to see how big Salvage Grande was. It looked similar to St Helena when I got closer. I was about ten miles off and sailing past all day. By evening I was still opposite the second island so I motored for two hours to try and get clear before nightfall. The wind came back gradually but was very light. I kept up 2 knots all night. This morning I found that I had gone a little too far to the west, so I set her on a more southerly course, which put me back on a broad reach. My speed has picked up to 3.5 knots. I'm about 110 miles north of Tenerife and will maybe sight land before long.

LATER

I've scanned the horizon for hours and haven't seen a thing. The nearest point is about thirty miles away. This happened when I was last here, the island was shrouded in mist. The sun is about to go down so I won't be able to see anything until morning.

The alternator doesn't seem to be charging the batteries; a bolt has sheared off the exhaust manifold which is blowing. Thank God I'm nearly there and will soon be able to do these jobs. I must try to save the engine to go into the harbour. The Mase is out in the cockpit, charging the batteries ready for starting the engine and supplying power to the electric anchor winch.

37

26 OCTOBER 1985

Land ho! I've been creeping up on it all night. At first I saw what I thought was a ship's stern-light but it didn't move and I realized that it was a light high on the side of the cliffs. As the night went on, more and more lights appeared all over the island. Now the sun is rising behind the volcano, Teide. What a beautiful sight! I'm four miles north of the lighthouse and very tired. I didn't get much sleep as I was adjusting my speed to arrive here at dawn. Last night I thought I could smell burning on board; I can smell it now and it's the smell of land. Dry, warm, parched land.

I've been trying to make radio contact with Jacqui La Lanne, whom I met on my last visit to Tenerife, but have failed so far. I'm worrying about all the work that needs doing when I'm ashore, but I always do this, worry like mad when I'm about to land. I get used to the daily routine of keeping the boat going, and suddenly everything changes. There are people, anchors, winches, mooring ropes and engines, and all that becomes more urgent. Out in the middle of nowhere, you can leave things until tomorrow if you want to.

The wind dropped as I got into the lee of the land. I had to start the engine as it was another thirty miles to Los Cristianos and I wanted to be there before nightfall. After an hour of motoring, waving to fishing boats on the hot glassy water, the engine started to knock and clouds of soot and smoke came out of the exhaust. The revs picked up and she raced away out of control. I throttled back and pulled out the engine stop which made no difference. Rushing down to the engine room, thinking that the cable had snapped, I tried the other stop with no success. Back on deck I tried to control the boat which was going round in fast circles. Suddenly the revs dropped back. I stopped the engine quickly and flopped into the cockpit, exhausted. Letting the engine cool off, I checked the oil, which looked rather thin, so I put in a pint and went back to trying to sail without wind.

After drifting for an hour I tried the engine again. This time it started immediately and purred away giving me 5 knots. I then motored for an hour and was getting close to Los Cristianos when the whole bloody thing happened again. Clouds of smoke, totally out of control, zooming around in circles, and then without warning she recovered. By this time I was a nervous wreck and extremely worried about taking the boat into the harbour. Jacqui had written to me saying that yachts were no longer allowed in but had to anchor in the bay, so I decided to go in and have a look and if it happened again, head out to sea. She had to cool off for ages before the engine would start and I motored gingerly into the bay. As I got nearer I saw that I could go close to the shore and, facing out to sea, anchor in between two yachts and still have an escape route. Finally achieving this, I switched off the engine, dropped the anchor, and poured myself a large Scotch.

I was well into my second glass when I heard a knock on the side of the boat. I stuck my head out and a voice said, 'I am Dennis Gale and my boat is registered in Aberystwyth. How about that?' Dennis has a trimaran, the *Inkwazi* which was registered only a few days before *Zane Spray*. We chatted away and enjoyed a few beers, then he left saying that he would pick me up in the morning.

After a good night's sleep, Dennis rowed me ashore where we encountered Mario and his crew, who had arrived during the night. They were amazed when I told them how long I had taken, as once they had left me, they had no longer sailed but had motored to Madeira, to Lanzarote and then Grand Canaria, spending a few days in each place. They took us out for a meal and thanked me for helping them at sea.

That evening Dennis and I met Jacqui at a friend's house. It was good to see him again. He volunteered to make arrangements to have my boat lifted out the next day, if I could get a tow over to the harbour wall. 'No problem, David, you bloody Welshman', he said.

The next morning Mario came over in his yacht, rafted up alongside me and towed *Zane Spray* over to the travel hoist in the small dock. Once in we had to wait for hours while the operators had lunch and a siesta. Eventually they lifted the boat out, mast and sails still on, and put me safely on the yard in line with the other twenty or so boats.

I took off the injector pump and gave it to Jacqui who knew of a firm at the other end of the island who could do the repair. Dennis, whose funds were running low, helped me in exchange for lunch and beer. Work proceeded happily over the next few weeks, but it seemed impossible to get the pump back. It was always 'mañana'.

A middle-aged English woman stopped by the boat wondering whether I took out charter parties. I immediately thought of Dennis and asked him if he was interested. He was, but didn't know what to charge or where to take them. Jacqui suggested a quiet sail to a sandy bay, a swim followed by plenty of cheap drinks, a cold buffet, and a brisk windward sail back to harbour. A few days later Dennis and I ferried six people over to the trimaran and in as many hours had earned enough to stock his boat for the Atlantic crossing.

People on boats have changed in the last few years. When I last came to Los Cristianos, most of them didn't have much money and worked in each port in order to carry on. This time I found lots of retired people with large boats doing the milk run over to the Caribbean, having spent years dreaming of palms and sandy beaches. By the time they get this far they find that it is not all blue water sailing and there is a lot of grey weather to get through. The more affluent, the less communicative they seem to be.

Dennis and I were having a drink on board after working late one night, when a beaming face appeared over the rails. He introduced himself as Herman Brinks, the owner of Sailomat, who had brought me out a new large rudder and heard that I was having problems with the steering gear. He arranged to check it over at seven in the morning as he had to fly back to Holland at nine. He was as good as his word and within half an hour had found the fault which was the piece of cord I had lengthened. The wrong type had been used and had thickened in the middle and become shorter as it worked backwards and forwards checking the wind vane.

People on holiday used to stop and say hello. One caller was the host of the Black Lion in Llanrhystyd. I was able to send two reels of film home with him for HTV. Another was a Scotsman who went back to town to buy me a bottle of Scotch when he heard about my voyage. I also met the son of a garage-owner from Llanon and asked him if his father had ever had a diesel engine that they couldn't stop. He told me of a tractor which had turned upside down. They righted it and started the engine, but were unable to stop it, as it was running on its own engine oil which had got up into the cylinders. It ran until it exploded. I did a very stupid thing when I put the breather pipe into the intake manifold. Although it got rid of the fumes and made the cabin smell better, it was running on those same fumes. I remembered giving Bert a tow over to the boat with the Mase in my Avon. I might have sunk him. What a horrible thought.

Richard Moffatt and his wife were planning a long cruise and needed experience in navigation and seamanship, and I had asked if he would care to join me in Tenerife to sail to Cape Town. Early in February he flew to the island, bringing my old wind generator and a gift of two solar panels from Chris Rudd. Richard and I worked at a reasonably average Spanish pace on the boat, finishing off all the repairs.

We did the last-minute shopping – bread, eggs, tomatoes, fresh fruit and vegetables – at a supermarket in the north of the island with a Tenerifian friend, Alvaro. After a long bus journey we met him in Santa Cruz and he took us to the supermarket where we filled two enormous trollies, spending about £150. We wanted a leg of ham, and as Alvaro seemed to be an expert, I asked him to pick one out for us. It was £45, rather expensive I thought as most of them were about £20. Afterwards we discovered why. It was wild boar. I asked Alvaro's girl friend where I could buy a mattress, and she said she had a spare one, five inches thick, four feet wide. She wouldn't let me pay for it, but asked for a kiss!

We filled up with water and diesel, and loaded the food. The boat was pretty shipshape and the anti-fouling done, except where the blocks are under the flat keel. We'll have to wait until the boat is lifted and quickly whack on a couple of coats, before she goes into the water. Richard and I need to leave Los Cristianos as we are feeling a bit land-stale, want to get on with the job and do some sailing. That's the reason we're here.

4

$\approx$

Zero Zero

We've made about seventy miles since leaving. Quite choppy during the night, in the shallow water. It's eased a bit now but unfortunately the wind has eased as well. Richard has been seasick and I'm getting pretty tired, having been on watch more or less the whole time.

A couple of hours ago I made a mistake. It was entirely my fault. The wind changed direction suddenly and I didn't have the boom under control. I was in the middle of a gybe, the wind died and came back with a bit of a snap. It cracked the boom. Not very good. The roll of repairs has started already. I took quite a bit of the mainsail off to ease the boom and there's probably enough timber to glue and clamp it. It's not an enormous problem. We could take the mainsheet straight to the deck.

I hope Richard starts feeling better soon. He's having a hard time and the seasickness tablets don't seem to be doing much good. He hasn't eaten anything, which I think is a mistake.

DAY THREE

The wind's been increasing all day. It started off about force four from the north-west and it's gradually gone up to force seven, so we may be in for a gale. It's giving us a rough ride. I'm trying to head slightly better than south-west because we haven't got that much sea room between us and Africa, about 160 miles. It's decreasing all the time, and if we head south we're not making enough west to curve around the Cape Verde Islands. I've been reducing sail all day. I've got her down to about 3.25 knots and pretty well reefed. We've been taking a few over the top and there is a lovely blue sky, with just a few puffs of cloud. A nice sunny day, apart from the wind....

DAY FOUR: 28 FEBRUARY 1986

Our position this morning was 24° 29′N 18° 12′W. We're not making bad progress, about a hundred miles a day. Last night we had a full-blown gale.

Richard had a coffee this morning but was then sick. He sat up for a while, but most of the time he lies on his bunk, unable to keep watch. If things don't improve, I shall have to pull in somewhere because he's going to become weak. I've tried to make him drink but he doesn't want to. If I have to put in, it would be either Dakar, or one of the Cape Verde Islands, the one with the airport. Isla de Sal, I think it's called. It won't be too far out of my way.

I saw my first Portuguese man-of-war yesterday, quite a large one close to the boat. We were going too fast to get any film, but hopefully I'll see some more when it's calm. They're beautiful to look at, a mauvish tint, like a big bag that's blown up into the shape of a sail. Underneath the water they have poisonous tentacles that hang down. They sail in the wind. I haven't seen any flying fish yet. There should have been a few on deck by now. I suppose it's a bit rough, but in rough weather they usually fly in big clouds. The tunny chase them and they take off on the top of the waves. I hope we see some soon, they are good to eat. I saw a Russian trawler; he went west to east, about 400 yards in front of the bows. I made a few clicks on the radio but he didn't respond.

On the ninth day in the early morning light the islands came into sight. Sal looked very barren from the sea. I sailed in close around the north end and then down the west side. Palmera was shown on the chart as a small fishing village with only a wooden jetty, so I was surprised to find a new harbour wall and a crayfish canning factory.

43

Sailing right up to the harbour entrance I motored over to a fishing boat and was welcomed by ten smiling islanders. The skipper waved me to go on the outside of him and the fishermen took the ropes and made me fast. I got out the remaining beer and we had a good drink and a laugh although we couldn't understand each other's language.

As soon as we hit the quay the colour came back to Richard's face. I have never seen anyone recover so quickly. He broke into a smile, couldn't get to the airport fast enough, and flew home the following night. I planned to leave the next morning, having gone 400 miles out of my way to drop him off. I had used the engine for ten minutes coming out of Los Cristianos and about the same coming to Sal so it must have used only about a litre of diesel. We had bought a lot of food to take us to Cape Town so the boat was much heavier.

8 MARCH 1986 AND STILL IN THE PORT OF PALMERA

Richard told me not to repay him for his share of the food, which was good of him. He decided to put it all down to experience. It will save him a fortune in the long run because I imagine he'll go home and sell his boat.

I've eaten a nice big crayfish given to me yesterday by Jorge Lopes Lima who exports live crayfish by air to Europe. He also runs a taxi and generously hasn't charged anything for driving me around.

I'm ready to sail. This afternoon a South African boy came down to the boat. He's flying home tonight and might have a problem at the airport. If so I said he could hitch a lift with me. I'm planning to leave in the morning. The boat is shipshape, nearly everything is ready. The bloody wind is screaming, it's blowing about force seven most of the time with big seas. Maybe it will be better once I'm a couple of hundred miles south. Oh well, you either get too much or too little. I took a last walk with the young boat-watchman, mostly in silence as he has no English and my Portuguese is restricted to 'bon dia, amigo' and not much else. Now I'm waiting for Jorge to take me to the airport to see the international police. They have my passport and the ship's papers and I hope there will be no problems.

DAY ONE: 9 MARCH 1986

Pounding into heavy seas, heading south-east, I set off at 11.30 this morning with help from Jorge and a few friends. I ran the engine for about five minutes, motored up into the harbour, while raising the main, bringing her about with half her sails up, switched the engine off and sailed out of the harbour. I was doing about 5 knots before I went through the entrance, which was very satisfying, and delighted the small band of friends on the quay.

I had a lovely sail down behind the island in the lee of the land. The water was quite flat and I was doing between 5 and 6 knots, but as soon as I came out of the lee the big seas started. I suppose the waves were about three metres high. I was ploughing into them, hoping to go outside the Ilha da Boa Vista about twenty miles south of Sal. I'm trying to cut through the channel between the two islands, not leaving myself on a lee shore as I go past. If there are any snags I'll have to run round the back of the island, which would be more of a struggle as I'd be on or near land during the night. Best of all would be to make a clear run of land before nightfall.

Last night I saw someone from the meteorological department who said there was wind coming from the north-east. There's a high up over the Canaries somewhere and the wind strength didn't look too great on the picture they had. They told me that the seas would be up to about three metres, so there's still a high sea problem. The glass has dropped back a little bit and is about 998 millibars, so I'm not clear of the rough stuff and into balmy, tropical waters yet.

DAY TWO

I slept from midnight until 04.00 hours and kept watch until dawn. My fix at noon put me at 15° 28′N 21° 44′W. Since coming out of the harbour and negotiating the islands I've done 125 miles. A good start. I'm sailing a pretty easy course and the seas have moderated a little, down to two metres, but there are two swells, one on the quarter and one on the beam.

I saw some flying fish today. Unfortunately they didn't land on deck, so there were none to eat, but I have just had a pot of Irish stew with a tin of peas thrown in, a nice meal. I recovered from my supper last night of sardines, mayonnaise, cucumber, cheese and ryebread. It made me feel sick which is hardly surprising.

Haven't seen any ships on this leg yet. I'm still bombing along at 5 knots on a south-east course, which will take me to about 300 miles off the coast by the time I am opposite Freetown. I will have to be careful in the Doldrums as I don't want to get barnacles on the bottom of the boat, especially now that I'm on my own. It's quite a hard job to clean them off at sea. I might have to motor-sail for a while if I get becalmed for too long. I've made up some long leads for the Mase, which has to be connected to the batteries when it is running, and put a pull-out connection in the middle of one of the leads. It used to make a big flash, which could be nasty if there was gas about.

I'm not too happy with the mainsail, and am seriously thinking of getting a slab-reefing main and an aluminium boom in Cape Town if I can afford it. It would mean taking off the mast and fitting a track to it for the sail slides. I'm losing a lot of power with this main and accept 4 or 5 knots when I should be doing 6 or 7.

The sun is about to set: only another quarter of an hour of daylight and I will light the oil lamp and start keeping a ten-minute watch, which means standing up and scanning the horizon for ships every ten minutes. I'll try to keep it up until midnight and then do the same in the early hours of the morning.

Good progress. I did 124 miles yesterday and it looks as though I will do another 100 today. The wind is much lighter and the seas have gone down considerably. The occasional big wave hits the boat. In fact one has just filled the cockpit to the coaming.

DAY THREE

Did a little filming this morning, perched on the side deck, trying to catch the flying fish as they took off from the waves in clouds, zooming all over the place. As soon as I got out there they all disappeared, and I saw what they must have been fleeing from as the fin of a shark came sliding through the water.

My course is south-east. I hope to reach a position two to three hundred miles off the African coast by the time I get to the Gold Coast. The currents are much stronger closer in to land and there are a great many pirates.

DAY FOUR

I am sitting in the sun wondering what I should do. Not very much comes to mind. It's still extraordinarily cool considering I'm only 12° from the Equator. The sun is nearly on the line at this time of year; the wind must be keeping the air cool.

Funny the thoughts you get when alone. I remember taking *Zane Spray* on her sea trials. I got through to the yacht club on the radio to ask them if they would send out the courtesy boat to take the crew ashore. They said they would be there in about five minutes. We waited, but nothing happened. I called them again and were told they could not find us. I gave them our position, the colour of the boat and left the anchor light on. Twenty minutes went by and they came on again to say that they had been right outside the harbour to look. I told them that there was no harbour at Abersoch, and they said, 'This is the Pwllheli Yacht Club!'

Later, on watch in the pilot house twiddling my thumbs, I had a hell of a shock. A bloody great flying fish fell straight in my lap. I've never moved so fast in my life. I was so surprised that instead of putting him in the pot, I chucked him straight out again.

DAY FIVE: 13 MARCH 1986

Position at 15.34 GMT was 10° 12′N 19° 16′W. Sal had constant high winds from the north-east, causing dust storms and covering everything with red Sirocco dust from the African desert. There is not a blade of grass and only a couple of trees on the island so it's quite dirty. I didn't get much chance to work while Richard was on board and the boat was rather grubby. I set to work and now the galley is sparkling.

I finally got through to Eric today. I don't think that he got my position as conditions were bad so they don't realize that I'm now tucked around the corner of the African continent. I'm heading for zero zero, and whether or not I actually make it there doesn't matter as long as I get to St Helena in one or two tacks.

I made a curry on my nice clean cooker. God it was hot! It started off with a garlic clove chopped up and fried with half an onion. I added some corned beef left over from yesterday, one tin of pie-filling beef, a small tin of tomatoes and grated carrot. Finally I put in some Spanish curry powder but it didn't taste very strong so I put in some more. It still wasn't up to my usual standard so I got out a new tin of 'Madras Hot' and shook some in. The boat lurched and a little extra went in, but it turned out fine. I have half a bucketful left over for tomorrow. Curries are always hotter the following day.

Had a hell of a job getting the Mase started today. It took me an hour, as I can only pull the start cord four or five times before needing a break to get my breath back. I cleaned the tank, the carburettor and the plug and eventually got it going. I hope it's not going to start playing up.

I hadn't run the engine since leaving the island five days ago. I'll have a beer and listen to the radio, as it would be nice to have a contact again. I'm alright, the boat seems in good shape and we've had a terrific run so far, covering 600 miles. Over 100 miles a day.

DAY SIX

I'm becalmed and have been adjusting sails all day, trying to get her to move and not getting anywhere. We are just wallowing, so I'll sit in the sun and have a glass of Scotch. When the sun starts to go down and it gets a little cooler, I will start the engine and motor away from today's beer cans, hoping that tomorrow will bring fair winds.

DAY NINE: 07.40 HOURS, 17 MARCH 1986

Very light winds. Yesterday wasn't too bad but now again I'm hardly moving. I'm still trying to edge around the corner, about two hundred miles off Sierra Leone, south of Freetown and on a good course. I suspect the current is giving me a bit of a lift to the south. The sun is just about slap overhead, it's pretty hot and over 90° in the cabin. I should be on the Equator at the time of the equinox. I hope that the winds get better when I pass over the Equator and into the south-east trades. It's slow going at the moment. My cruising chute isn't really large enough, only 400 square feet. My staysail is 350 square feet so there is not much difference between them, although the chute doesn't slat as much. Buying a much larger chute somewhere on this voyage is a priority.

DAY TEN

Nothing much happening. The wind came back and the wind generator started to turn but not for long. Two jobs done. I cleaned the carpets and silenced the two sheet blocks on the side decks. They have been driving me crazy. One is right above my bunk and every time the sails slat the block hits the steel deck above me. Now they are lashed around the shackles and so can't fall over. What peace! I wonder why I put up with it so long?

I'm still just about moving, but because the log is faulty it isn't showing any speed, not even 0.1 of a knot. It was pretty depressing seeing only 2 or 3 knots on the clock when I was making 130 miles a day. It would be nice to know how fast one is going, even to see 0.1 up there sometimes would be encouraging.

DAY ELEVEN: COMING UP TO 04.00 HOURS IN THE MORNING

No wind last night and I'm sitting here wallowing with slatting sails which are taking a lot of wear and tear, chafing as they flap and crack backwards and forwards. Had a visit from some dolphins and a breath of wind from the west so I went back to sleep for a couple of hours. It wasn't a very restful night with such a racket going on.

Still a long way to the Doldrums. I will have to be at least 2° south of the line before getting any decent winds. It's taking rather a long time, but one is not able to sail without wind and I can't motor around the world. Some people don't understand that although the diesel tanks are quite big, the range is fairly limited. One can't go bombing off, flat out, without a tanker following.

I meant to get up early and motor for a couple of hours before it got too hot but when I woke the sun was high. The navigation lights were still on and the batteries flat, but a very light wind came back and I'm sailing very slowly in the right direction. It's very hot but there is a lovely breeze coming off the mainsail and through the main hatch into the cabin. I was feeling rather dodgy this morning so took some salt pills as the heat has suddenly intensified. Only five days ago I was still wearing a jersey at night.

I think I had another visit from the dolphins today. I heard a loud splash in front of the boat, but all I could see was a large circle of oily-looking water where something big had gone down.

49

DAY TWELVE

Still drifting along slowly at half a knot on the cruising chute and full main. I got up in time to run the engine for an hour before the sun got too high but this heated up the whole boat. The weather is changing: a lot of electrical activity in the sky last night and flashing ahead of me.

I checked the engine oil and it's rising again, which means that diesel is still getting into the oil. Hell! I'd hoped to do some motoring to get out of the Doldrums but don't want to ruin the engine. It was a bit smelly this morning. I wish the diesel would leak somewhere else and not into the oil. The fault must lie in the injector pump seal leaking back into the sump. Maybe I could relieve the pressure by taking the diesel return pipe back to the tank instead of to the fuel filter. Perhaps I can get some help with it in St Helena. I built a good powerful engine, she runs smoothly and fumelessly until she starts filling up with diesel. At sea I can only change the oil and, if it gets too bad, sail for Ascension. I'm sure the Royal Navy would be pleased to help.

I'm in the middle of a thunderstorm. It's rather nasty all around – thundery, Doldrums weather. I was standing in the main companion-way when a great flash came, followed almost straight away by a bang, nearly knocking me back into the cabin. The wind is still light, I'm doing only 0.5 knots and heading towards a really black area. I hope I can stay well behind it. One of the worst thunderstorms I remember at sea was off St Dogmaels, Cardigan Bay. There was a terrific squall that came from nowhere, several of our boats were going back to Aberaeron in heavy rain with visibility of only a few yards, the fizzing sound of lightning hitting the water and the crash of thunder. Some poor guy got killed on the beach: he was sitting on the sand and the lightning struck his watch. I have great respect for the energy up there. I don't like it, but I treat it with awe. I think it's great, sitting comfortably at home looking out of a window at rain, lightning and howling wind. But out here you have to take whatever decides to come.

I have just sung:

If you want to go to heaven let me tell you how to do it,

Grease your feet with a little mutton suet,

Slide right out of the devil's hand,

And slide right into the Promised Land.

Go easy,

Go greasy.

I think it made me feel a bit better.

It's time to unplug the antennas on all the electrical equipment. If I am hit but don't sink then I would like the Sat. Nav. and radios to work. The last five minutes have been indescribable, but nevertheless I'll try. It started to rain, so I got the shampoo, dashed out into the cockpit and had the most gorgeous shower I've had in my life: unimaginable, after six days of sweltering heat. Last night I bathed in salt water, using only half a pint of fresh to wash off the salt. Oh, to stand out in the rain, the cool rain, probably 70° but it felt so cool!

Another flash, rather closer than the last one. It had quite a boom after it and I'm off course again. The wind is playing up a bit; I suppose it's bound to be all over the place at the moment. It's fantastic: we are racing along at 6 knots on the cruising chute. The sea's absolutely streaking past, flashing of lightning everywhere. The whole sky is lit up from horizon to horizon and sometimes I hear enormous bangs and crashes. The wind generator is buzzing away like mad. It's exhilarating to be on the move at this sort of speed again. Fantastic stuff! The rain is good and I feel great. I don't like lightning but this wind is amazing, right on the quarter. I'm heading on 160°, the course I would have chosen if I'd had a choice. Another Lucifer. I don't know how long it will last but it's nice.

DAY THIRTEEN: 21 MARCH 1986

A terrific night's sailing with thundery squalls and heavy rain. She kept ploughing along and I've put in a few miles overnight. This morning the wind went completely, and I'm rolling on a mirrored sea under an overcast sky.

12.55 HOURS

Still waiting for the wind and my radio contact. I tried to sleep but it's so bloody hot, steaming hot, the sweat just runs off you. I have only the chute up now, which spends most of the time wrapped around the forestay, on a hot, flat, glassy sea.

A little sail in the night, a maximum of 1.5 knots, but pleasant. I stayed up to enjoy it and save batteries. I'm feeling a bit down at the prospect of another couple of weeks of this before reaching the Trade Winds. It was a crazy idea to come this way against the Trades, but I didn't imagine that I would be bogged down so long in the Doldrums. When I left the Cape Verde Islands I thought I was going to average 100 miles a day until I got around the corner, followed by a few days drifting along to zero zero.

It's a bit of a problem without the engine. It would have been nice to put in ten miles a day motoring while the wind is like this. Not that it makes much difference apart from morale. I've been working steadily all day, swapping from one tack to another, putting the cruising chute up and then taking it down at the slightest wisp of wind, out in the blazing sun for an hour at a time trying to get her moving.

DAY FIFTEEN

Had a contact with Paul Orton in Edenbridge, who is going to ring Eric to give him my position. After breakfast I threw a Weetabix carton over the side and have just passed it again. It must have been going faster than me, or perhaps I have been sailing in circles.

There is the merest gossamer breeze, just enough to fill the chute: not registering anything on the log, but I am moving. The lack of progress is beginning to wear me down. I took seasickness pills this morning as the motion was making me rather queasy. Had a nasty pain today, starting as cramp in my shoulder blade and going right through my chest. It's hard work handling the sails; I don't know how many times I have done it in the last few days. I don't mind when there's a puff of wind and the sound of the ripple of water on the sides of the hull.

At 04.00 hours this morning I woke to find I was sailing the wrong way, not very fast, in fact hardly moving, following the moon. I got out on deck, worked out where the wind was coming from, turned the boat around, handed the chute and the main over to the other side and, before I knew it, was sliding along at 2 knots.

This evening I had just finished eating some boar's leg, onions and potatoes, when the wind changed suddenly from the south-west to the north-east, and for a time I was doing 7 knots. It's lighter again now but there is a big thunderstorm to the north.

During the night I heard the throb of an engine. I realized that he was about to go ahead of me and watched his lights and listened to the dunk, dunk, dunk. I hadn't realized how close he was until I saw the black shape of the hull slipping by some 200 yards ahead. I tried to raise him on the VHF but he just plodded on his way, and I wondered whether he had seen me. If we had been aircraft it would have been a near miss, or a near hit, whichever way you like to look at it.

DAY SEVENTEEN: 25 MARCH 1986

I'm at 03° 35′N 11° 38′W. I have never worked so hard in my life, etching my way, inch by inch, and am beginning to feel the strain. Not a glimmer of wind from anywhere and clouds building up. I've handed the chute over to the other side yet again as I saw a ripple on the water half a mile away. It's 86° in the cabin and I'm melting away. I had a look over the side earlier, leaning out as far as I could on the bow. Barnacles have already started to grow on the bottom, just what I don't need. I feel rather despondent and won't try to come this way again, ever. Ten days of Doldrums so far.

Lots of activity but not much progress on the following day. I've been through an oil slick, the sides of the boat are covered with thick black tar to about six inches above the water line, and to make it worse one of the sheets was hanging over the side. I had to cut it free, let it drift away and replace it, as it would have got tar everywhere. Even a simple job like collecting water in a bucket on the end of a rope is difficult without getting plastered in the stuff.

I spent the morning fighting with the cruising chute, trying to untangle it from the forestay and finding it twisting in the sock as I tried to pull it down over the sail. I've stowed it away in the cabin and hope to sort it out by the time that I need it again.

I hardly dare admit it but the wind has been coming from the south for about four hours, the first time for ages that I've not had to rely on thunderstorms and black weather to bring it. Could this be the start of the south-east Trades? It has come up nice and steady with plumes of cloud rising in the sky to the south. I'm still on a south-westerly course trying to make some south and letting the current take me towards the Bight of Guinea. At the moment the log is showing 3 knots; I don't know what that is in real terms but if it keeps up I could do a hundred miles in the next twenty-four hours. I will start up the fridge in a couple of days to cool the champagne for the Equator celebration. I'm out of Scotch, vodka, and gin and there's not much beer and wine left either. There is something that feels like a bottle of Scotch. Ann left it on board for my birthday and I think there's a packet of peanuts with it. I will try to wait another twenty-four days before opening it.

DAY NINETEEN

So much for being so cocky. The wind went at 17.00 hours last night. It was nice while it lasted: six hours of good sailing and it looked as though it was going to stay. I need 10° more to the east before I can break through and do a bit of stiff sailing against the south-east Trades. At the moment the problem is breaking through the Doldrums. A couple more weeks of this and I'll be a stark, raving lunatic. I can imagine seamen becoming unpeeled in the old days. It's so hot and in a week I've moved only 120 miles, or something like that. It's getting worse and I'm finding it very difficult to do anything. I try to sleep at night as it's too hot during the day. I can't sleep in this temperature.

One mile south and two miles east so far today. I managed to make some north last night – how the hell, I don't know, I don't understand it. Oh shit, this is awful! It won't seem so bad when it's over, it never does. I'm trapped here. With a working engine I could be motoring for two hours morning and evening, but without I have to sit it out, even if it does mean another two weeks on the Equator. I must be going doolally. It's difficult to think straight in the doldrums. I'm certainly not able to.

I boiled the boar's leg to get rid of some of the salt and it's much better. In a minute I shall cook some spuds and peas and get stuck into it. I don't feel like eating but know I must.

I ran the engine in the evening cool, to charge the batteries and put a pipe from the breather out of the aft-cabin hatch to keep the inside of the boat clear of fumes. Within half an hour smoke started pouring out of the cabin. A small leak of diesel was coming from one of the injectors and running down the block and this, I thought, was causing the burning and fumes. A few minutes later the steering wheel vibrated and the revs picked up a bit. I switched off, and down in the smoke-filled engine room found that I had burnt out all the belts, the whole bloody lot, they were lying in shreds all over the floor. They must have been slack and only needed adjusting. Luckily I have another set of five on the shaft ready for an emergency but I mustn't do that again, it was just plain bloody stupid. So another steaming-hot, nasty job is awaiting me down in the engine room.

The wind has come up lightly from the east and I'm moving forwards. I've had a moonlight visit from some playful dolphins and could hear heavy breathing not too far away. I can't think what it was, but it had a bit of power behind it and must have been quite big. There is a lot of thunder and lightning in the sky to the north. I stayed up until midnight and she was just ticking along. I slept soundly and don't know what woke me but by the time I got into the cockpit she was doing 6 knots and really shifting. I thought I should reef but it started to rain heavily so I first closed the hatches and portholes. By now she was doing over 7 knots and I was in a bad squall with the lee scuppers well into the water. I tried to get the jib in first, letting a little of the sheet off, but the sail started to flog. I couldn't budge the furling line so I let off more of the sheet and the force of the wind pulled it out of my hand. I started to furl it in, still flogging, and above the howling of the wind heard a ripping sound as I finally got the sail away. I let the main sheet off and found a preventer still tied to the boom which I had to cut as I was unable to undo it. The thunder and lightning was all around me as I crouched naked in the bottom of the cockpit praying for strength to pull the wheel over and get her off the wind. Out of the corner of my eye I could see 8 knots on the log, as she hammered along out of control. The lightning seemed to be striking the aft deck. She wouldn't come off the wind, I tried to furl a bit of the staysail and on the second attempt got about half of it in. Up she came, I furled half the main in and a few minutes later was running down the wind at 5 knots, back on the self-steering.

Every now and again, working in the pouring rain, I could see something hitting the aft deck and flashing but was concentrating too hard on the job in hand to take much notice. I had never before been so unconcerned about lightning and was worrying more for the safety of the boat, as at one point it looked as if I might lose control of the situation. When things quietened I took a look at the aft deck to find that the flashing had been the strobe light in the Dan Buoy which had broken loose and was rolling around the deck. During the panic the chute started blowing out of its bag which was lashed to the side deck and being sucked into the water under the boat. I hauled it back, bagged it and got it into the aft cabin. By then I was so tired that I shut everything up and slept for two hours.

I was up again, still tired, at seven o'clock. As the wind wasn't too strong I got the jib off and put it down below. It's now in the fore-cabin with the jib sheets, absolutely knotted. It will take a month of Sundays to undo them. I filmed the jib while up unfurled with the ends flying.

29 MARCH 1986

Big event coming up in a minute. I've been waiting for it for half an hour. I don't know how accurate the log is but it has been showing 4,400 and something miles for five days and has just reached 4,500.

A busy day and now I am absolutely knackered. I put four of the belts on the engine, tensioned them, lined them up and did everything else that I could do in that department. I had a good wash as I was pretty black after working in the engine room. The seams on the jib are glued together, ready for sewing and most of the patches are on.

Three weeks at sea today. The first week was terrific, the second not too bad and the third's been hell. I shall have to give up the idea of going to zero zero. I'm stuck. Absolutely stuck. If I can make west and south-west I shall, and if not I must sail back into the Atlantic to find a wind. I've been sitting here like a duck for about a week and however hard I try seem to end up heading for the African coast.

The Ivory Coast isn't the place that I want to be and I'm nearly going to pieces. My psoriasis is bad, I have a heat rash and feel generally uncomfortable. It's been very tough. It's hard being becalmed and trying to repair things, like the sail I've been working at all day. I must do another bit later on, but it seems endless. It would help if I heard Eric's voice on the radio; we haven't been in touch for two weeks now. I've used two gallons of two-stroke already, charging the batteries, but think there are still five left. But only one bottle of beer!

I'm losing sea-room now and this bloody coast is no good to anyone.

56

Around the Ivory Coast there is often trouble with pirates who come out in small boats to attack shipping. I don't know how far off I am, perhaps about 150 miles, so I must concentrate on sailing out of trouble instead of where I want to go. And if I've got to sail north and west back into the North Atlantic, I've got to do it. I'd then have to see if I have sufficient water and supplies. I'm facing the prospect of another thirty days before reaching a safe harbour.

When I opened the sewing machine a fly flew out. He must have been there since I was in Los Cristianos, hibernating perhaps. I don't know how long he'll last – the flies that came with me from Sal died within a few days. I had a bit of a massacre to try to clear them out and then, lo and behold, they disappeared, the whole shooting match. They may not like salt air. This guy's a bloody nuisance and keeps on landing on me. Only one fly, but I'm going to kill him, poor bugger. We're out here on our own but I still don't like him settling on me.

EASTER SUNDAY

I'm becalmed again and feeling desperate. I need to make more than 2 knots to get away from this current. It's taking me north-east, so I've got to do something. It is upsetting me now. It took me twenty-one days to get to Cape Finisterre and the same to reach here, but this time it started off so well. It would be easier if there were two of us, easier to get the work done, to make decisions, and good to have a bit of company. I shed a few tears. It's so depressing, wallowing here, knowing that tonight I'm going to go north-east again, unless I get some wind. The cruising chute is up, and I'm going the quickest way I can – if I go too far north-west I might as well go home. I've thought about that a lot today, wondering what the hell I was doing, sitting here on my own at Easter, sweating in heat of 90° or more, lonely as hell. Why? What for? This is a down patch, really down. I can't motor all that far, I can't rely on using the engine.

A bit of wind at last! I went through a fit of swearing and cursing and stomping around the boat which cleared the air a bit, and then I prayed, and the wind has come. It has come from the south-west, which means that I can steer south-east. Not the way I said I was going, but the best I can do.

I drank the last bottle of beer today. I'm running out of stuff rapidly now, nothing essential but it's nice to have a glass occasionally. There's always Ann's birthday present but I'd like to hang out until the 19 April. Don't know whether I'll last that long.

DAY TWENTY-THREE

Spent the whole night trying to see what would happen if I sailed to the west. Nothing happened, I hardly moved. April Fool's Day tomorrow, my granddaughter's birthday. I wish I could be with her. A good wind this morning, 3 knots on a south-east course, so I hope I can scratch away from the coast. I feel absolutely knackered. I have been struggling with the sewing machine all day and managed to finish the sail. It doesn't look very tidy but I think it will be strong enough. A lot of loose stitches kept appearing underneath the sail and several needles broke, which was worrying as I don't have many. Perhaps it was the thicker cotton I was using, having run out of the usual one. I can't put it up yet as I am too tired. Whenever the needle broke, it meant going out to the cockpit, stopping the Mase, going back to rethread the machine and out again to restart. All because I was worried about using so much petrol.

I'm back on the port tack and heading slightly south of west. It's been blowing about force four most of the day. It's overcast, dull, cloudy, very hot, but I'm moving away from the coast and that's what I want.

Last night I stayed up until midnight, slept for four hours, put the lights out and kept watch until dawn. Before falling asleep I noticed that, instead of switching off the navigation lights, I had in fact switched on others, and rather than saving battery power there were several others blazing away. It would have been better if I had stayed in bed.

Haven't seen the fly again; he's either hibernated or snuffed it. Poor little fellow waking up all those miles from home! I'm out of beer, but there's wine, and the bottle of Scotch that I'm trying to be strong about. No contact on the radio over the weekend; it would have been nice to get through. I've a headache – it must be all that sewing.

APRIL FOOL'S DAY: 06.00 HOURS

It's howling out there, thunder and lightning, another squall. I took some sail in, but not much of the main. It's still dark and I only hope that it all holds together. I've let the boom right out to spill some wind, trying to keep her on a quiet course. The rain is streaming down. It's one thing or the other.

I've now reached 03° 06′N which is the latitude I was on four days ago. This is the way I originally intended to come and the wind has let me plod this far south, while the current takes me to the east. It's still overcast.

DAY TWENTY-FIVE

I was becalmed all night, managed to sleep most of the time and appear to have drifted about six miles back to the north and not to the east. This contradicts the charts, which is peculiar; maybe under certain weather conditions there is a different current. I woke this morning to a clap of thunder and a few flashes of lightning, so went out and had a shower. Now the wind is taking me to the south-east, and at the moment she's doing fine.

Got through to Eric at last. I could hardly hear what he was saying but it was good to hear him, and I told him about the engine and sails and that I am being drawn towards the Gold Coast. The batteries are now pretty flat and will need charging again today.

13.45 HOURS

Becalmed, pointing in the right direction but drifting backwards. I'm at 03° 09′N 09° 55′W and have already slipped back two miles to the north and to the west. God, I can't stand much more of this. It's boiling hot again, over 90°. I'm very sore with a sweat rash although I have plenty of fresh water showers when it rains. It's so hot that I'm coming out in sores. I managed only twenty-odd miles in yesterday's lovely little sail, but at least it was in the right direction.

I really need a bit of luck. Two or three days of good winds to carry me down to the Equator, across to the south-east Trades, and then I could do something, then I could sail. Not sweating away here, using up water, stores, and getting nowhere. Sooner or later I'm going to have to make a decision on whether to motor out and take the chance of ruining my engine, or put up the cruising chute and sail north-west into the Atlantic again, because I'm going to need stores, strength and materials to keep myself going.

DAY TWENTY-SIX

I'm clawing my way back, three miles south again, another six miles and I'll be back where I was the other day. I kept sailing all last night but with not enough speed to register on the log. This morning has been the same. I awoke to a lot of thunder and flashing, so reefed right down and waited. Of course nothing happened, so I set all the sails again and am now waiting nervously for what comes next.

I had three large sacks of bread sliced and toasted at the bakery in Tregaron before I left home. It will keep for years as long as it's airtight and dry. I put some under the grill and have just had it with tinned tomatoes, a good snack. I'll make some fresh bread when things are more settled and the temperature goes down.

I took the solar panels off and checked them over but couldn't find anything wrong, so perhaps it was a bad connection. They are back on again and seem to be working all right. The sun isn't right on them yet so I will have to check them later on.

DAY TWENTY-SEVEN

A good start. I had put off running the engine for long enough and as it is a bit overcast and the batteries are down to 11.5 volts, I decided to run it for an hour. The steering was balanced nicely so I carried on without a problem and was able to sit in the cabin, as there were no fumes.

I am a bit of a fool sometimes. I can design and make things but am not always able to use them. Because the log is not showing the correct speed I have been trying to keep up by putting more pitch on the propeller blades, which has strained the belts and engine. Today there have been two hours without problems and cool air has been wafting through the boat. The oil level came up a bit but I have enough oil for one change and could use the spare water pump to extract it from the engine. After I switched off, the wind came from the north-east – little white horses, blowing about force four, thundery and stormy-looking.

No matter, I'm on an easy course. My position is 02° 50′N 08° 48′W; perhaps after all the boat *wants* to go to zero zero.

5 APRIL 1986

Twenty-eight days from the Cape Verde Islands. It seems as though the boat hasn't given up, she's edging across and down; I have very little to do with it, it's almost as though she's programmed. The water supply is holding up. I put in a lot of purification tablets in Tenerife, so it tastes strongly of chlorine, like drinking out of a swimming pool. It's rather nasty so I'm boiling it which gets rid of the taste.

I have just cooked the best loaf of bread ever: it's turned out beautifully, well-risen, enormous. I made it in the washing-up bowl and put it into a black plastic bin liner out in the sun to rise. As it heats up the bag blows up like a balloon and doesn't touch the rising dough. At this moment I'm eating warm new bread with margarine on it, oh it's beautiful, the first bread I have made on this voyage.

DAY TWENTY-NINE

My midday position was 02° 08′N 07° 07′W. I motored for two hours as it was overcast, and was sweating and becalmed until 16.30 hours when the wind started back. I don't know how long it will last, but it's here, and to be moving again is incredible.

I had just finished an enormous sandwich for supper, took the plate out to the cockpit to wash it in the bucket and looked up to see a bloody great trawler about 300 yards away. I put a pair of pants on for the first time in weeks, got on the VHF and had a talk to the skipper. They had come from Germany to fish off the Namibian coast. They sped close by at 15 knots to my 4 and I went on deck to wave and take photographs. I can't get over the excitement.

DAY THIRTY: 7 APRIL

A fantastic night, most of which I've spent sailing at 4 knots. Not only am I moving but heading straight for zero zero. I shall start a new chart, as she is determined to go down the line. A couple of birds are flying ahead of me. They were on the water and I disturbed them. This is great stuff – on the move at last! At four o'clock this afternoon I had been sailing non-stop for twenty-four hours; haven't had anything like it for weeks.

DAY THIRTY-ONE

This is a marathon. A lovely stretch of sailing followed by twenty-four hours of hardly moving. I'm still drifting eastwards on the Guinea Current: every now and then I get a little breath, move forward and stop again. I made more loaves today, splitting the dough in two as I think they will keep better. It's a real scorcher out there. That's the beauty of having a pilot house. When one is sailing the breeze funnels down through the open hatch but it's pretty hot when one's not. A breath of wind. Just moving, eating the miles off gradually. I need only two good days to do the 300 miles to zero zero. I'm not in command at the moment: the boat and the wind are.

DAY THIRTY-FIVE

Five thousand and nine miles on the log now, which must mean something; I shall have a cup of coffee and play patience, it's too hot to work. There are thunder clouds building up all around me. It's now 13.30 hours and no wind since early this morning. I saw a line on the horizon, raced to reef the sails and tried to set a new course for when the wind will hit me. There's nothing more terrifying than seeing a line of white foam advancing over still, glassy water. The hull gives a groan and lists, the sheets and sails creak as they stretch, after flapping so long. I race along wondering if she is ever going to stop accelerating, praying that it will level out at 7 knots, and then suddenly one is back to 3 knots and wishing that it would last a little longer. I've made a bit of progress, but it looks as though I'm now in the counter-current. I wanted to cry this afternoon, everything's beginning to get me down. I felt that if I could cry it would have made a lot of difference, but I couldn't find any tears. Instead I stormed up and down the decks, swearing and shouting for some wind, and in the end I got my tin whistle and blew that. To whistle at sea is a superstition, for fear of whistling up a wind.

DAY THIRTY-SIX

Wind and rain, doing 4 knots, well reefed down. I was sailing nicely all morning on a path between thunder storms, one to the east and one to the west. All was going well until the one on the east disappeared and before I knew what was happening I was swallowed in a big black cloud as one thunderstorm was engulfed by the other. I had a shower and washed my hair while I was reefing the sails. The wind gradually built up and was blowing gale force for about an hour when it settled down to a steady force five to six. The sky looks very angry.

DAY THIRTY-SEVEN

This could be Equator Day as my position is 00° 26'N 01° 58'W. I'm not heading straight for the line but trying to make as much east as possible. I might need it later. No contact with the outside world. I'm wasting battery power listening every hour for Eric; contact must be established again sooner or later. It won't be so bad when I know what time he's going to call.

5

The Cape of Storms

DAY THIRTY-EIGHT: 15 APRIL 1986

I'm over the line, I'm over! The longest I have sailed single-handed. I had a champagne breakfast and got the camera out, but before I was ready a tuna jumped four feet clear of the water, flipped over and landed back head first. What a sight! It will stay in my mind for the rest of my life, clearer than if I had got it on film. I stood there in amazement with the camera pointing to the ground.

17 APRIL

It looks like the North Sea in winter at the moment, nice and hot but pouring with rain. A large breaking sea is coming from the south and I'm thrown about quite a bit when the wind goes light. I am feeling depressed about the lack of progress which may be due to a lot of stuff growing on the bottom of the boat. I can see grass around the water line if I lean over the side. It's impossible to know exactly how bad it is without getting into the water, and it would have to be very calm for me to be able to do that.

19 APRIL 1986

My fifty-sixth birthday and the first one on my own. I opened the present that Ann had left on board and, as I had thought, it was a bottle of Glenfiddich and a packet of hazelnuts. I'm playing patience like mad. I didn't play on my first voyage, or during the times spent in hospital, but now it's becoming a habit.

I've just seen an albatross. Under 2° south of the Equator. It's odd how they stay on this side, I've never heard of one being sighted on the north. I love to see them, such beautiful birds with big hooked bills and an incredible wing-span. In the evening cool I cut a Guinness cake saved in a tin for the occasion, lit the candle and enjoyed a slice with a couple of glasses of Scotch, outside in the cockpit. I'm in a happy mood.

DAY FORTY-FOUR

I'm at 02° 21'S 00° 44'W. Started the Mase up this morning, as the batteries were down, and fifteen minutes later there was an almighty bang. As soon as it had cooled I stripped it down and found that the coupling from the engine to the alternator had disintegrated. There is nothing I can do but wait and see if I can get one made up or sent out to St Helena. I won't be able to use power tools or run the engine much and may have to go without lights at night.

I tacked this morning. The course wasn't good but gradually improved, and in the afternoon rain started to tip down. Until nightfall I tacked first one way and then the other in light flukey winds and rain. It is nice to get her settled to a course before going to sleep but it doesn't look as though there will be much peace tonight.

DAY FORTY-SIX

A lovely wind until an hour ago, when a large black cloud appeared from nowhere and the wind died, leaving me in a large slopping sea. The main chafed as it flogged backwards and forwards, pulling some screws out of the track on the boom. Something else to tackle. I should put the sails away when it's like this but always think the wind will come back; it never does.

After a lot of thought I tackled the Mase. I used a battery terminal, the type with a bolt attached to take the wires. I clamped it to the shaft but it rattled loose when I started up. There was still a lug left on the original casting, so I drilled and tapped a thread inside it with a hand-drill, screwed in a bolt with nuts as spacers, found some rubber pipe about the right size, and after a struggle got it all assembled. It's running on only one pin but sounds fine and it works.

When the rain stopped the wind finally came back from the east, which has given me a good fast course to the south at 6 knots. During the night it came round until I was heading south-south-west and I covered fifty miles, which made a nice hole in the distance left. The mainsail outhaul broke just now: more work. If I can only keep her together for a little longer I will have cracked sailing against the trades to St Helena.

DAY FORTY-EIGHT

Bombing along – I shouldn't say it yet, but I am. When I woke at 04.00 hours the sails were backed and she was facing the wrong way. It was probably a lull and she must have gone through the wind in a circle. I put her back on course, a beautiful sky, little puffs of cloud, real trade wind stuff with breaking crests on the waves. I'm ploughing over them. I've enough power in the sails to push her on at a good speed, averaging 6 knots, which should give me a good day's run. The wind is cool enough to stand in the sun naked. If this keeps up for a few days I'm right on course. However, I must not count my bridges before they are hatched.

DAY FIFTY

Another good night's run. I spoke to a ship from Scotland this morning. They gave me a barometer reading, as mine was way out, and told me they could see me five miles off on their radar, which is reassuring.

DAY FIFTY-THREE

I moved the ham radio from under the chart table, where it was likely to get splashed, to the deck head above. I had added some wires as there were too many joins, so I ran a heavier piece of cable. Leon Dalziel, another radio contact, had told me my signal had a bit of warbling on it and thought it would be low battery power or high resistance in the wiring. I have tried to eliminate both.

This afternoon she has slowed down. The course is still good but I could miss the island by up to sixty miles, which will mean either a tack to the east or a run past and a sail back on an easier course. I might get there on Saturday, but I hope not too late as the boat wouldn't be cleared by customs. A pity, as it's on Saturday night that all the action takes place. The pubs are full and noisy games of dominoes and cards are in progress. You might think that a language other than English was being spoken, sounding like a mixture of Cockney, Wiltshire and Welsh. There are only three pubs in Jamestown. In one there is a cool courtyard. The girls work in the hotel upstairs and peep through the windows and giggle as they look to see who is new in town. When the pubs close everyone heads for the village hall to dance. Everyone dances: it doesn't matter how young or old.

DAY FIFTY-FIVE

Had quite a blow last night, unusual for these parts, big seas. I was bombing along, crashing into them, uncomfortable but making good progress. I'll be glad of a rest after the bashing I've had against the trades. I'd dearly love to see land now, to smell it and to feel its warmth.

Fifty-six days at sea and 'Land ho! Land ho!' They must be able to hear me on the island, the way I'm shouting. The third of May 1986, and I've done it. Against the Trades to St Helena. Thirty miles ahead there's a bloody great big lump on the water. I've bloody well done it, all I need do now is to get in. What a beautiful day!

I motor-sailed, to round off the course and sail closer to the wind. The seas were rough and spray was flying everywhere as we headed for land. I had to go through some steep overfalls and at one point, when we were thrown off the top of a wave, the engine missed a beat. I wondered why, and an hour later, approaching Jamestown Bay with the sails neatly furled away, the engine stopped. I think I had picked up air and had an airlock. The sea was nice and quiet in the lee of the island, but the set of the current seemed to be taking me towards the steep cliffs at Rupert's Bay. I got the Avon dinghy and started to inflate it thinking that I might be able to tow *Zane Spray* with the outboard motor to the safety of the bay and pick up a mooring. I was pumping away, running out of time, and got through on the radio to the Island

Fisheries. I told them what had happened and asked if they could give me a tow in. They said there would be a fishing boat back in two hours' time. I explained that by then I would be on the rocks, and within five minutes four smiling fishermen were with me in a 20-foot wooden boat. It took them an hour to tow *Zane Spray* on to a mooring, even though I helped with the sails whenever we had a breath of wind.

The place has changed a bit; sometimes I think it's not good to return. It was nice to see old friends, but since my last visit the cinema has been closed. Because of the collapse of the rand, sterling is now worth twice as much as before. Everyone has bought videos, cars and motor-bikes.

On my first night ashore I went to Ann's Place, a fish and chip restaurant in the corner of Jamestown's beautiful shady park. St Helenian fish and chips are little to United Kingdom taste as the fish is tuna and the batter has hot red pepper in it. Sitting at a table on my own, I quickly made the acquaintance of the owner and crew of *Rode'orm*, from South Africa, and after our meal I introduced them to the delights of Jamestown: all three pubs and on to the village dance. They were subsequently very helpful to me, scrubbing the bottom of *Zane Spray* and doing all the mast work, and on their last night invited me on board for dinner.

One morning I met Douglas Wallace, the owner of a tuna cannery, who had settled some years ago on the island after sailing from England. He offered me a bed as, having sailed himself, he knew how nice it is to stay ashore when possible. Over a pint of beer he suggested that I should call back on my way home, making St Helena the point I cross on my homeward track. The miles sounded shorter as the beer flowed and I agreed to try.

The local engineering firm repaired the Mase, making a new part for only £5. They are very innovative, the islanders; they have to keep things going, as with no airport it takes ages to get parts sent in.

It was evening three weeks later by the time I had got on board the food for the next leg of the voyage. The crew of another yacht helped me cast off the mooring lines. I motor-sailed down the lee to the south-west, the wind was coming off the land and it wasn't long before I turned off the engine and was sailing close in under the towering cliffs. The next morning I was surprised to find myself going slowly in the right direction, but just astern was St Helena in nearly the same position as when I had gone to sleep. I must have been becalmed all night.

The plan is to head south-west, and try to break through the Horse Latitudes. In the days of square-riggers, although horses were one of the most valuable cargos, they were the first to go over the side when becalmed. They drank a great deal of water. Once through these latitudes I would carry on south to pick up the westerlies on the top edge of the Roaring Forties.

DAY THREE

A terrific wind from the west all night, so I'm steering a course to the south-east, which according to the charts I'm not supposed to be able to do. As the day wore on, the wind came around to the south-west, but now that the bottom of the boat is clean I can still manage to hold south. After three weeks without sailing I had forgotten how to work out the magnetic variation. In this area it adds up to quite a lot.

I noticed that there was a tear in the staysail, only three inches long when I first saw it but nine inches by the time I had got it furled away. The wind had more or less died so I dropped the sail and sewed away like mad by hand to get it finished and up again before the wind got too strong.

We've covered 130 miles in the last twenty-four hours, which I'm very happy with. It would be nice to make a quick passage. It's easy enough to run down the Trade Winds, but to go against them feels like a real achievement.

DAY FIVE

Not a good night, becalmed on and off. When the wind came it was in strong blasts that lasted for a short time only, and it was back to slatting sails until the next time. Have done a few jobs around the boat, nothing too strenuous. I was advised to switch on the engine and motor through the high, to save myself five days or more. The Horse Latitudes are usually between the tropics and the westerlies, but I would have to motor for 100 miles to be sure I was through, and I can't face doing that. In fact I can't face switching on the engine. I don't know what's wrong with me. There were so many problems at the start of the voyage that every time I use it I think it's going to mean a lot of extra work.

Suddenly at 19.45 hours, after waiting all day, the wind came up from the south-east. I'm holding a course of south-south-west, not bad at all. It's amazing that a clear blue glassy sea can change in five minutes to small white breaking crests. I sighted three whales this afternoon, about half a mile away. I filmed them using the long lens, but think I got only the water vapour after they had blown. Whenever they surface I'm facing the wrong way and see them going down.

DAY SIX

Since the wind came up last night, I've been streaking along, it's absolutely marvellous. I'm pretty well reefed down, half the jib and staysail and three-quarters of the main. Beautiful big blue seas and a wild-looking sky with long grey wisps of cloud and dazzling bright sunshine. Doing a good 6 knots, dancing over the tops and then crashing into the next wall of water. I do find this rather tiring, not as wearing as being becalmed but very noisy, and one's body is on the move the whole time. The wind appears to have gone around a little more and I'm nearly heading south.

Not long before I'm out of the tropics as my position today was 20° 18′S 03° 55′W. The solar panels seem to be working alright, but the Mase sounds rough. The rubber pipe I used for the bushes is perhaps not strong enough, maybe alkathene would be better.

5 JUNE 1986

I have been trying to slow the boat down, to stop her slamming into the seas. I need to get some rest as the last twenty-four hours have been physically exhausting. I've made a good leap forward and am still to the east of St Helena. Not bad. I just hope that I'm through the Horse Latitudes now.

I was listening to the BBC World Service 'Outlook' programme and heard them mention that I had sent them a letter from St Helena for the UNICEF Stamp Appeal. I covered the envelope back and front with stamps of all values, leaving only a window for the address, and it's got there already which means that Gillian might get the card I sent for her birthday.

Seven thousand miles on the log today. The mileage seems to be fairly accurate, unlike the indicated speed. It is about 6,000 miles to Cape Town from the English Channel, but I must have put on an extra 1,000 miles going to zero zero. The sea has flattened out and there is a large swell coming on the nose from the south-east.

DAY TEN

Gillian's birthday. My course and speed are good, but disaster strikes again. After a poor QSO with Leon in Johannesburg I found the batteries well down, so decided to run the engine for a bit. When started it had no drive, so I switched it off. To my horror the key had come out of the small pulley and had been spinning and wearing the shaft out. It had been one of the jobs I had done in St Helena, as the welds on the pulley carrier had begun to crack. It must have been slipping while I motor-sailed out of Jamestown Bay, when I would not have noticed it. I hope I've fixed it. I found a piece of thin stainless steel tubing that was once on the milking machine at home. It was the right size when I split it but it took a long time to get it together again. I heated it with the blow lamp to expand and then tighten it, and then, to make sure, I ran over it with epoxy glue. Hopefully it will hold until Cape Town. Another claw ring has broken off the mast, leaving only the bottom one. I must make the rig and engine reliable on my next stop, as these two let me down all the time.

DAY ELEVEN

A lot has been happening. I'm not able to think clearly but I'll try to get it down. About an hour ago I saw a weather front approaching and I went out to the cockpit to gybe her on to a new course and reef her down before things got too nasty. Halfway through the gybe the wind hit the boat sooner than I expected, with such force that the boom crashed over, breaking it in two. One end hit the rails, the other smashed into the top of my head, knocking me into the bottom of the cockpit. The splintered end writhed backwards and forwards above as though it were trying to stab me. Trying to collect my wits, I let off the topping lift which was holding up the other end of the boom. Still dazed, I got the mainsheet off, putting it on to the clew of the mainsail and set a fairly safe course.

71

I'm sitting here feeling not very well with an extremely painful back, a five-inch cut across my head, and the boat screaming along out of control. I don't think I was knocked out as I seem to have got things done. There's a bit of a gale, blowing like mad. I'm stiff and sore and it's very painful. On course for Cape Town, too much sail up and she's a bit lively for comfort, bombing along. I can't do any more.

DAY TWELVE

A beautiful night which started off slowly. I got up at 03.00 hours to find her off course. I goosewinged her straight as an arrow downwind, without too much rolling. I'm still not feeling too good but combed some of the matted blood out of my hair. Yesterday was wasted. I spent the day with the boat well reefed down to keep her safe until I felt stronger. I'm concerned about the mast which will take all the strain without a boom. I put out more sail this morning and the speed picked up to 5 knots straight away. I'm only forty-six miles from Greenwich Meridian. It will be the first time on this voyage that I have been east of Greenwich.

DAY THIRTEEN: 10 JUNE 1986

My position is 27° 12′S 00° 18′E. I'm over the line and on course towards the African coast at Orange River, a thousand miles away. I've repaired the mainsail furling gear and taken the gooseneck off and what was left of the boom. The boat is in fairly good order again, but for fear of straining the mast I tend not to push when I do have a good wind. The barometer has been rising all day and I've got a nasty feeling that I'm getting stuck in the middle of a high pressure system, the southern high, which should be far to the north by now.

DAY SIXTEEN: FRIDAY THE THIRTEENTH

Things are pretty quiet, in fact bloody quiet, heading east until the wind went around. I was holding a course to the south-south-east and doing 4 knots until it went light again at dawn. A nice smooth westerly wind would suit me, would waft me in. I could make it in five or six days and do 130 miles a day again. I need the wind to be free, either a broad reach or a run, a nice strong, steady wind right up the chuff.

But with what I've got at the moment I could be another couple of weeks. I don't want to use the engine because of the problem with the pulley. It would be nice not to have an engine and no question of whether or not to switch it on. Or off. You'd be totally committed. If you're going to use an engine you might as well motor round the world.

Did some filming this morning of an albatross. I hope it comes out. I used the close-up lens. It was flying around the back of the boat and has been with me for quite a long time. They are difficult to film.

The World Service has just read my letter:

Dear World Service,

I hope this envelope comes in handy and that you have a good auction for UNICEF and raise a lot of money.
I'm a disabled sailor trying to go around the world in a small boat that I built myself.
I listen to the Beeb a lot on my travels but would find weather reports helpful for the areas I'm in – usually they seem to be about Outer Mongolia.
I wish I could spell.

Yours,
David Sinnett-Jones

DAY SEVENTEEN: 14 JUNE 1986

It's Saturday and I'm becalmed and have been becalmed all bloody day. The wind comes up every half-hour, I move forward 200 yards, then it bloody well stops. Oh Christ, I don't know. My position is not very far from yesterday's. I sailed a bit overnight and it doesn't look too bad on the chart. But today so far has been bloody impossible.

Made some bread and boiled some spuds and generally arsed around all day. I slept well last night and woke up at daylight. The hurricane lamp had run out of fuel and gone out and the navigation lights were still on. Maybe it's the bang on my head. Certainly I have needed a lot of sleep in the last few days.

About 850 miles still to Cape Town. The barometer's dropping a little which probably means I'm in for a gale. I am in a bloody awful mood. Perhaps the wind will come up and I can waft my-

73

self to Cape Town in five days. I've done only about 350 in the last week.

DAY EIGHTEEN: 15 JUNE 1986

It's Sunday and my prayers have been answered. The sky started to clear from the north-east last night and the wind came back lightly which meant I could pick my course nicely on a broad reach. The wind is on the quarter now and I'm haring along. It's so much easier running downwind because the boat isn't under pressure, unlike beating into the seas. Everything's under pressure then, including the skipper.

16 JUNE 1986

In the end the wind came up as a front, changing direction rather suddenly. I managed to swap tack to keep on the same course. The rain hit, we carried on slowly, reefed well down but in the right direction. The wind stopped until about 05.00 hours, absolutely not a breath. I was left in large breaking seas, rolling and banging all over the place, a most uncomfortable night.

The wind was at about force two this morning until we were doing 5 knots – it was beautiful; and then over in the west a black cloud appeared below the top of cumulus looking really nasty. I reefed down and waited and wondered if I had reefed too soon because we nearly stopped. Eventually the rain came and when it hit I wished I'd reefed more. The boat was totally out of control for a few minutes. I was standing in the pilot house, still dressed in my heavy weather gear, wondering what I should do and – wham – she was nose down ploughing through the water at 8 knots, spray flying everywhere, waves coming over the top, beetling along, absolutely crazy. There was no point in going out to reef more, the wind would have torn the sheets out of my hands. I just had to pray and stand there and watch until there was a lull, and then reef quickly which felt a bit more comfortable. I was still doing between 4 and 5 knots in the right direction until hit by another couple of squalls. The wind dropped and I put the sails out a bit more, when up it came again and I put them straight back in. I'm just trying to hang on in here. It's the middle of winter in the South Atlantic so I'm bound to get some rubbish. Things would be easier with a crew, as one could always be on watch while

74

the other was resting. I tried to sleep but it's no good until this settles down.

DAY TWENTY-ONE

My position at 14.00 hours was 30° 75′S 9° 42′E. I had a good day's sailing until about 22.00 hours when the wind dropped and once more I was stationary. It came back this morning from the north-west. I've had a beautiful day running with the wind on my quarter, doing about 6 knots, pretty good. A few clouds and dark patches but, once they were over, then nice and clear. The sun is very bright down here in the Southern Ocean, a sort of white light. The glass has dropped a bit, but seems to have steadied out, so hopefully I'm not in for another blow. The last one lifted me on my way quite merrily but was a bit tiring.

THURSDAY

This morning's position is terrific. I'm still running with the wind full on the quarter doing between 5 and 6 knots. It would be nice to get in without another gale. If this lasts another four days I could be there. Straight downwind, terrific stuff.

It will be great to get to Cape Town and have a meal, a few jars at the yacht club and make some telephone calls. I'm not too sure whether to declare the film at customs when I arrive. There is a state of emergency at present and it might be thought that it is banned newsreel film which would drop me in the shit. I'm looking forward to a break, having stopped only three weeks in St Helena. I could have done with a month, but need to get to Cape Town as there is so much to do on the boat to have her ready for the Southern Oceans: mostly work on the mast, boom and sails. And I want to spend some time with my daughter Madeleine in the Transvaal.

Not doing too much, just standing here watching her bomb along; it makes a nice change from pinching courses, to be able to sail anywhere that I want. I could go straight downwind but that would be a little more uncomfortable, so I'm keeping the wind on the quarter. Oh, that's interesting. There are two albatrosses trying to mate in mid-air. They are landing on the water now: maybe they thought that it wasn't such a good idea!

It's 20.00 hours and dark. There's a real hooley blowing out there; it's been building all day, but has really turned into a gale tonight. She's well reefed down and making 7 knots. I am worried about the mast and sails but it's nice to be covering the ground.

DAY TWENTY-FIVE

I'm trying to be patient; had a good night's sail yesterday and the night before, but not quite on the right course. I'm heading for Cape Columbine which isn't where I want to go. I need a wind change. My position this morning was 31°59'S 14°33'E, about 250 miles from Cape Town but too far to the north. I will have to tack. The glass has gone up to 1022 millibars, which is quite a leap from yesterday at 1009.

Christ! This is the last fucking straw. The wind is coming from the south-east and it's moving all over the place. It doesn't matter where I tack, I'm all right for five minutes, then it goes off and I have to tack back and the same thing happens again and again and again. I'm so bloody close, 200 miles from the African coast. The wind is so light that on the other tack I go slightly north of east. I get it right some of the time but when next I look the wind has gone around 10° and I have to tack again. I'm very frustrated. I know I can't do anything about it and it's bloody awful. Everything looked absolutely perfect for a good run into Cape Town. With hindsight I could have gone a little more south a few days ago and could have picked any course that I wanted, which would mean that now I would be heading east.

Yesterday I pumped up the fenders, put the courtesy and quarantine flags up on the spreaders, and generally got her ready for going in. Now it looks a long way off. I am a pain in the arse. I would just like to get in there and have a nice glass of Scotch in my hand. I haven't had a drink for at least three weeks. Clouds still forming in the north and west, wisps in the sky.

DAY TWENTY-SIX

Half-past three in the morning. I woke to find my prayers had been answered. I woke with the wind in my face. Conscious of being becalmed for an hour or two and hearing the boat slopping about while I was asleep I realized that the wind was coming through the hatch. I thought I must have gone around, or that the sails were backed, and got up to find the wind had gone to the south-south-west. Once again I can plot a course straight for Cape Town. What a relief! A beautiful calm sea, moonlit night, a few puffs of cloud about, and a steady wind. Three knots and under way.

DAY TWENTY-SEVEN: 24 JUNE 1986

The wind stopped this morning and has been farting about all over the place again, light and completely in the wrong direction. I'm heading south as I lost ten miles to the north last night. I could motor in, but the pulley is a problem and it's just not worth taking a chance. It would mean standing at the wheel for two or three days.

The earliest I could get in would be tomorrow afternoon. Had a good QSO with Leon last night. Madeleine has been worried – that's the trouble with the radio: once you lose contact people start to worry. Yesterday afternoon I was creaming along between 4 and 5 knots, but last night and today – nothing. Every day now is making me more and more desperate.

I saw a passing albatross. If I had wings I could be there in five hours, they glide along at about thirty miles an hour, absolutely effortless, such beautiful birds. Some small Cape birds have joined me. I remember them from last time, but not what they're called. Also some white birds, a kind of streamlined seagull, but nicer looking.

Still heading southish in a very light wind, doing about 2 knots. Hopefully I'm making a bit of east but I'll have to wait and see on my fix. Saw a ship this morning about four miles ahead going north. Nothing else has happened, except that I washed my hair in fresh water, getting ready for shore leave. Once more.

Just tacked again. I'm going up and down and up and down. This morning I was about 145 miles off and I suppose I'm still about the same because I went south – I can just make south on the port tack; on the starboard tack I make below north-east. A half-knot current is coming up from the Cape against me, affecting me on both tacks, which means twelve miles a day off the course I'm steering. Everything is stacked against me and there's not a damned thing I can do about it. If I thought that I could use the engine, I'd use the engine, but I can't face another repair job a few hundred yards off the bloody beach.

If I was going straight round the Cape to Australia, it would be easy:

77

I could sail around with no problem at all. It wouldn't worry me. It's just that once you make up your mind to go in somewhere you start champing at the bit. If Madeleine was not waiting for me I'd be tempted. I could go south until clear and would be bound to pick up a westerly which would carry me on to Australia. At least I think so. Oh well, I've got to do my mast, and a lot of other work on the boat before taking off from Cape Town. A lot of things need doing for comfort. The engine compartment should be boxed in and silenced and the companion-way steps done. I have put up with an old Second World War 303 ammunition box instead of steps for long enough. I shall build them so that they are a protection from spray and have two sides which one can grab hold of.

If I had an Autohelm I would probably use the engine more. I could play a game of cards while it's plodding away and wouldn't have to look after it the whole time.

DAY TWENTY-EIGHT

I've been becalmed since 06.45 this morning. Absolutely bloody well becalmed. It is written in the log: 'One hundred and twenty miles off the Cape of Storms. Becalmed.'

Oh, I need a wind for twenty-four hours, a free wind, that's what I need. I've got to get it, it's got to come. I've been saying this all day and it comes up from the north, it comes up from the south, comes up from the east, comes up from the west, comes up from every bloody place, just a puff, and then nothing. It's a beautiful scorching day, an absolutely clear sky, the barometer has gone down a bit but not too drastically, and the sails are slatting and wearing themselves out. The skipper's wearing himself out too. It will take two nights and a day to get there if we take off now, if the wind comes now, and today is the twenty-eighth day. I will have been within 200 miles of the coast for a week. I've been out shouting at the bloody wind to come because I'm . . . I don't believe it, it's gone again.

I had good radio contact with Leon last night, which cheered me considerably. Madeleine had rung the Royal Cape Yacht Club and Dinky in reception remembered me and was pleased that I'm coming back. They are going to keep an eye open for my arrival which was supposed to be yesterday. I've cleaned the gas cooker, I've cleaned the saucepans, I've baked some bread, done all my washing, done everything I possibly can, but I can't rest if the sails are slatting. The sun shines in my eyes every five minutes and I think I can feel a breeze so get up and adjust something.

It gets dark quite early in the evening. A ship has just gone past. And every now and again 0.1 of a knot comes up on the log – I'm sitting here watching it, on a good course. I'm not sure where the wind's coming from. The sails are still slatting and flopping around, but let's hope it's the beginning of something. I've been sitting here since six o'clock this morning; it's so frustrating to be so close. Let's hope I can get sailing soon; that's what it's all about, not sitting around like this.

DAY TWENTY-NINE: 26 JUNE 1986

Very light winds during the night. I think I managed about twelve miles. I'm about a hundred miles off now and there's no wind. I've put the cruising chute up, having thought I wouldn't need it again on this stretch but I'm not moving yet. The wind is from the west now, it doesn't really know where it wants to come from. All over the place. Rather like I feel.

Still no wind; I've had a puff now and again, handed the cruising chute from one side to the other and another mile has appeared on the log. I threw some paper over the side and in about a quarter of an hour it was 500 yards behind, so I am making some progress. It's difficult to keep the boat on course; I have to check every few minutes because there's not enough wind to operate the wind vane.

I've just seen the strangest thing. A fish, about nine inches long, swam past the boat with its head out of water. I'm not going mad, it kept lifting its head right out of the water, putting it under again, swimming a bit further and up with its head again. A sitting target for a bird. I've never seen anything like it.

13.30 and I'm on the move. I'm not too excited because it's happened so often before, but I'm doing about 2 knots on the cruising chute and three-quarters of the main. A nice free wind, quite long swells but a flat sea like glass with little ripples as the wind comes up and on the top of each swell a calm patch.

That didn't last long. I spent the afternoon becalmed.

DAY THIRTY

Thirty bloody days. Sixty miles off and we've gone slightly north overnight. The wind is going around in circles and there's thick fog. I'm very tired. I cried, prayed, and finally could stand it no longer. I put the belts on the engine and started to motor. There's a jangling noise but I think it is going to be all right. Going along at a steady 5 knots, and then up to 6, I realized that the wind had come up and was giving me a lift. I switched off, adjusted the sails and found I was doing 3 knots on course for the Cape. My prayers have been answered.

The barometer was still dropping and by the time it was dark I was in the middle of the shipping lanes. The wind was free and I could pick my course so I headed in closer to land to go down the coast about five miles off. The wind was up to force six now from the north-west and ahead of me I could see a glow of light in the sky: Cape Town in the distance. By that time I was so tired that I badly needed to sleep. Two trawlers seemed to want to fish exactly where I was sailing. I dodged them for half an hour and then gave up and slept with my alarm set for the hour.

As always when one needs a fix the most, there never seem to be any satellites going over. I made sure that I had enough sea-room to clear Robin Island, and by dawn found myself a bit too far to the south. I could see Table Mountain and the Apostles in the grey morning as I sailed straight in towards the harbour.

Closer in, I realized I was too near Green Point and would have to come hard on the wind to make the harbour entrance. I could have started the engine, or turned and sailed south to Hout Bay, but carried on and scraped my way half a mile off to the sound of waves breaking on the shore.

I knew that once around the main breakwater and into harbour there would be a free wind to sail the last two miles through the docks to the yacht club, where Bobby Cattermole, the marina manager, would be waiting to tow me in. I had asked the harbour authorities to find out whether he could tow me the last few yards into the marina. Rounding the corner of the entrance I found a police launch waiting. It came alongside and I was told that they had come to take me in tow for the last two miles. Having managed to sail that far I wanted to sail right up to the marina, but felt I couldn't turn down this kind offer. If I had, 'Sod's Law' being the way it is, the wind would have stopped or gone around to head me.

On my approach the tow was swapped to Bobby on the yacht club tender. There were lots of helpers to take my ropes, nudge me into a berth and make me fast. It was still only 09.30 hours on a windy but fine Saturday morning and somebody shouted, 'The bar is open, David!'.

6

Good Hope to Cape Leeuwin

Having removed my Henry Lloyds and put on some jeans, I made my way unsteadily to the yacht club bar, where great interest was shown in both boat and voyage. I wasn't allowed to buy drinks, which came faster than I could manage them. I made and met both old and new friends that morning and one, Ray Harper, offered to look after *Zane Spray* while I went to visit Madeleine.

I borrowed a bottle of Scotch from the club and ordered dinner at the restaurant before returning to the boat to sleep until the evening, but when I woke late that night the yacht club was closed and every one had gone home.

After arranging for the boat to be put on a safe mooring, Ray drove me to the airport and I flew to Johannesburg to stay with Madeleine, to be thoroughly spoilt for six weeks. While there I met Leon, my Afrikaans contact, for the first time. He was a representative for Transvaal Motors, travelling a great deal. He consequently took me with him to show me the countryside.

Six weeks later I returned on the Trans-Karoo train, which took twenty-four hours to make a 1,000-mile journey. It was wonderful to travel all that way by steam, through such contrasting landscapes: from the dry flatlands of the Karoo, with small square gun-towers where the farmers made their last stand in the Boer War, to the high snow-covered mountains, across deep valleys on trestle bridges, down to the lower wine-growing valleys and back to Cape Town.

Ray met me at the station and took me to the post office, where my new Autohelm and spare parts were waiting. I was told that I would have to pay tax before taking delivery. Every country in the world, including South Africa when I was last here, classes parts for a yacht in transit as tax-free. I discovered at the Customs House that this is no longer the case. I spent the whole day in that building, covering most rooms on the six floors, and not until I got to Room 153 did I have my first glimmer of hope, when the man sitting behind the desk smiled and said, 'You have to be a yachtsman coming here at three on a Friday afternoon.' After I had explained my predicament he told me he would sort it out and sent me to another floor for a tax evaluation. There I was greeted by the most obnoxious bastard that I have ever met. He took great pleasure in telling me that the import tax could be either 40 per cent, or only 10 per cent if he regarded it as safety equipment. I explained that I was in transit, that the goods were being exported and were therefore not liable to tax. At this point he decided to make it 40 per cent. Telling him that I would have the parcel sent home and then on to a more reasonable country like Australia, I stormed out of his office and back to Room 153. The man with the friendly face wrote 'tax exempt' on the forms and took me to another office, to get them stamped, where we were told that this was not allowed but, looking to the sky as if asking for forgiveness, the official smashed the stamp down on the forms and my heart started to beat again.

I ordered a new three-point slab-reefing main, had the old main recut as a jib, and new clews fitted in the jib and staysail. Ian Davidson, a member of the yacht club, drove me to a timber yard which had a good stock of Douglas fir. I needed this to straighten and fill in the back of the mast. They cut the pieces to size and delivered them to the boat.

I took the diesel injector pump off the engine and stripped down the front end to have a look at the seal, finding a corrosion line from where the diesel had been leaking all this time. I went to a manufacturer to ask the price of a new part, but it was so expensive that I found an engineering firm to hard-chrome and machine it at a quarter the price.

Ian invited me to a barbecue and out with some of his friends. We sailed out of the harbour to a shipwrecked tanker near Robin Island. The ship has a hole the size of a double-decker bus in its side. Ian said half-jokingly to one of the guests, Jennie Muir, that as she hadn't much on at the moment, she should sail with me to Australia. I hadn't considered having a woman as crew member and we both felt embarrassed at the suggestion. Later I met her in the yacht club and she offered to help with any necessary painting.

After a few weeks the crane lifted the mast off *Zane Spray* and placed it across some forty-five-gallon oil drums in the boat yard. I set about the task of straightening it, routing out the back, fitting and glueing-in the new back section, and finally planing it to a tapered round shape. Jennie rubbed it down and varnished it. She worked hard and seemed to enjoy herself and, remembering Ian's suggestion, I asked if she would like to sail with me as an expense-sharing crew to Australia. She was delighted with the idea, but first had to let her house and get her finances in order.

In the next few weeks we beavered away; the boom arrived and then the sails. I ordered a lot of plywood and made steps for the main companion-way to the pilot house and then a floor in the passageway. This led to the aft-cabin past the open engine room, and one would no longer have to walk on the sloping bottom of the hull. I cut the rest of the plywood into the useful sizes I would need to complete other jobs at sea.

Ernest, a likeable Zulu, helped me paint the decks. He worked hard to please his new benefactor – I was paying him twice the going rate for the job. The only trouble was that I had to keep my eye on him, not to make sure that he was working, but to keep ahead of him and cover everything that didn't need painting with masking tape. While working in the pilot house one day, I saw him sitting on deck, dabbing away with his brush and talking to two friends. I asked Jennie to translate and apparently he was telling them of how he had risen in the world, commanding a much higher wage than most for his skill in painting. I liked Ernest's smiling face and still think of him when I look at *Zane Spray*'s decks.

The BOC Around-the-World Race arrived at the end of the first leg. The South African, John Martin, in the yacht *Tuna Marine* came in first, to the delight of the local crowd. There was much excitement in the club for the next few days as the rest of the boats came in.

On Wednesday 22 October 1986 Bobby and Ian cast off our mooring ropes and we motored out of the marina. Ian, with Jennie's twenty-one-year-old daughter Nyali, followed us out to sea in his yacht. Once in open water I stopped and we hoisted the sails. Ian motored alongside,

rately searching for forward drive as I motor out to sea.

David thinking, November 1932.

My bossy sister, Ann, teaching me to swim. She wasn't so successful with spelling. South Beach, Aberaeron.

dwarfed by the hull as it starts to shape.

hining the propeller parts on the ord M7 lathe.

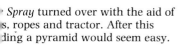

Spray turned over with the aid of s, ropes and tractor. After this ding a pyramid would seem easy.

Zane Spray by the cowshed, ready for painting.

Just hold it there boys. The light's not qu right.

Stuck by the milk stand, trying to reach t sea. After leaning on a few telegraph pol and with the help of three tractors, we fin made it to harbour.

ay of the launch. I
d until late evening
e tide to come in
aw her float for the
ime.

e faces. Ann (on the
Gillian and me on
ay I'd hoped to
, 15 September

The following day. Still blowing hard from the south-west. And still waiting.

Advice from Sir Geraint as I start my voyage.

In the first few minutes I learn how the Sailomat works.

My view for the next three years.

Pidgey in the cockpit look rather sad.

Whales who had just rub shoulders with me.

Sitting at the chart table, listening to music as the become calmer.

passing over a bottle of champagne in which we toasted each other. They wished us *bon voyage*, we waved goodbye and sailed on the light south-east wind to the west to get a good distance from land by nightfall.

DAY THREE

Jennie has been seasick but seems to be getting over it. She's eating, and helping around the boat and I reckon in another day or so she'll be fine. I have also felt a bit queasy occasionally and it's been fairly rough, with nasty choppy seas after a quiet start. We've been beating into headwinds to try and get south of the Agulhas. This is our third full day.

The boat is much quicker with the new main. Now that I have three-point slab-reefing I can drop and reef the sail three times. Everything leads back to the cockpit. That stop cost a fortune and I'm quite pleased to be off, as the bills were horrendous. Poor old Gillian is going to have bills coming in for the next few months. However, the boat had to be fit for the South Atlantic. I was pushing my luck with the mast as she was.

Haven't seen any ships for the last twenty-four hours, bar a few fishing boats when we were on the edge of Agulhas. The boat is going beautifully. I'm doing 6 knots in spite of two reefs in the main, and as soon as the seas go down I'll shake the reefs out and we'll bomb along.

DAY FOUR

The antenna wire on the port side of the mast had broken so I unplugged it and went back to the whip antenna that I used originally. No radio contact until today when I heard Eric talking to Leon. I shouted like mad but they didn't hear me. Perhaps conditions will soon improve.

DAY SIX

We had our first gale on day five. For a day and a night it was blowing like mad. I cut one of my fingers fairly badly when taking a rope out of the stopper. It pulled my finger into the jammer and took a bit off around the nail. The gale came up from the north and we were flying along, going great guns, making east about fifty miles south of the tip of Agulhas Bank, not in the deepest water but on the 100-fathom contour. We were still sailing at about 3 knots but at the next satellite fix had dropped back several miles. I imagine there is quite a strong current as during the next two hours we lost another six. I changed course with great difficulty. When I went to check the weather helm the wheel felt very light and I asked Jennie to turn it while I looked at the cables in the engine room. They were alright, so I dug around in the aft-cabin locker looking for where the quadrant is supposed to be. There wasn't a quadrant any more – it had exploded and broken into pieces. During the gale the rudder must have been swiped by a large wave, breaking the quadrant as the wheel was locked in position. It's very annoying as it was specially manufactured for boats of this size. Steering the boat has been a problem. Luckily the wind changed and I managed to get her on a course heading south last night. The current still pushed us back but at least we're making south.

A bolt had come out of the furling gear on the jib, and last night the strain broke the control line and unfurled the sail. I tied it up to the rails and now we've only got about half the staysail, but we're still managing to do about 4 knots most of the time.

At the beginning of the gale I was goosewinged. I had three reefs in the main which was too much, so I decided to take it down. I let the halyard off but the sail wouldn't come and I had to go to the foot of the mast and pull it down physically, while Jennie controlled the line at the other end. She gave me the boat-hook, enabling me to manoeuvre it above the sliders and pull down the main. It was difficult because there was so much weight of wind in the sail trapped up against the rigging. I must put a downhaul on the head of the mainsail so that it can be pulled down as well as up.

DAY SEVEN

I've given a lot of thought to the problem of the rudder. Making a new quadrant seems a bit ambitious in the middle of a gale. I put a snap shackle on a piece of rope and attached it with some tape to the boat-hook. When the weather calms down I hope to be able to get it hooked on to the loop welded on the back of the rudder and lead the rope back to the cockpit for emergencies. I could steer by pulling one rope or the other. I have to get some form of steering back: we would never get into harbour at present.

We met a Chinese fishing boat last night, slightly to my starboard bow. I switched on the radio and he asked what course I was on. I told him I had difficulties with the steering. He was still dead ahead and I set the Sailomat and passed close astern of him. He must have been trawling very slowly and probably didn't want to move. It was rather hair-raising as I could have been caught in his nets.

DAY TEN: FRIDAY 31 OCTOBER 1986

Our position this morning was 39° 47′S 22° 39′E. Jennie and I went on to the aft-deck to see if we could clip a rope on to the rudder with the boat-hook. The Sailomat oar was at right angles to the water and something was definitely wrong inside it. It was impossible to attach the rope to the rudder as it was too far under water and not clearly visible. I will have to put the ladder over the transom and go down and get the rope attached. Having no steering gear at all, I rigged up a temporary outfit in the aft-cabin using blocks and tackle to pull on the little bit left of the quadrant.

Waking Jennie at about two o'clock in the morning, to use the first light, I dressed in my wetsuit and we tied the ladder to the aft-rail. I took the Sailomat to pieces and found that the plastic link had not broken, but for some unknown reason the oar was out of position. I couldn't work out what to do, but thought I'd better finish at least one job. I went down the ladder and Jennie fed me the ends of the rope which I passed through the hole, getting half of it up, then tying a knot and pulling it down into place and repeating the operation. The water didn't feel too cold, but it was quite hairy hanging on to the stern with about two miles of water underneath me. Jennie hooked one end below the Sailomat and picked it up with the boat-hook. With the ropes leading back to the sheet winches in the cockpit, winching up on one rope and slackening off on the other, I could turn the rudder to steer a better course.

Absolutely shattered, I went to rest. As I took my suit off the cold hit me. I was freezing. Jennie filled empty wine bags with hot water and packed them around me in my berth. I had hypothermia and it was hours before I regained a normal temperature.

Later we dressed in our heavy weather gear and had another look at the Sailomat. The boat was tossing all over the place. If I turned the oar around and pushed it downwards it would go back to the right position. Unfortunately the plastic coupling had come off, so we had to put the oar in the right place and get the plastic link back underneath the mechanism. The rudder and oar tend to turn with the seas, and one's fingers are liable to get trapped. Eventually I managed it, using string and gaffer tape stuck underneath the clip, and pulled it into position. We managed to bolt it back on and within three-quarters of an hour had it all done. We reconnected the lines, set the Sailomat, and the course changed straight away. It was perfect. Now the boat can be steered on just about any course.

I must try to make a quadrant before reaching Perth. Once in calmer waters and more organized, I shall cut out the pieces and bolt or weld them together. It should be possible to make up something more permanent that will give us some sort of steering. We'll need it to go into harbour or up river or even to drop anchor. Maybe a local blacksmith will make something, or another part could be flown out.

DAY THIRTEEN

A good old blow again last night which gradually came up until I was doing about 5.5 knots. This morning the wind went and then came back again from the same direction. The barometer's down to 995 millibars which is pretty low. I wonder what is next in store for us? The Sailomat seemed to be moving around so I checked that all the nuts and bolts were tight. They were, but the transom is flexing. I had put another stop cord on the wind vane, which had come off during the night.

Jennie has made a string net to put the vegetables in, which we will put up today. She's settled in fine and keeps a good watch. I hope to teach her to navigate and handle the boat on her own. She's a very good cook and it's great having company on board.

I think I broke a rib when working on the Sailomat. Something went crack and I find it quite painful when lying down and getting up. I think it's the fourth rib up on the right-hand side.

DAY TWENTY-THREE: THURSDAY 13 NOVEMBER 1986

Our position is 36° 18'S 39° 22'E. Hearing a lot of noise from the transom, I went to have a look at the self-steering gear. The rudder on the Sailomat had worn away on the inside of the break-tube and was rattling backwards and forwards, juddering and crashing about. We got out the spare rudder and lashed the ladder on to the transom again, having first failed to do it from the deck. I got down into the water, started the rudder in position and then had to hammer it up into place, as I couldn't get enough leverage. Very tired, I came back on board and got the boat sailing on course.

The following day I was still not at all happy with the way she was sailing. The small spare Sailomat rudder is not as powerful as the one that Herman brought out to Tenerife and it wasn't coping at all. After a day sailing the best course under the circumstances, I looked to see what was wrong, and the plastic break-link had come adrift. We took it all to pieces again, lying on the aft-deck and hanging over the rail, got the link back in and put it back together, which took about an hour and a half in a violent sea. Jennie passed me the tools as I asked for them. Having been becalmed for about five hours, as soon as I got on the ladder the sea started to come up. The wind blew a howler, sea was splashing everywhere and I was nearly knocked off the ladder – always the way when one starts a job like that.

While taking a large wave over the side, one of the foresail reefing lines was washed down the cockpit drain, out under the boat and then caught around the propeller so badly that the engine could not turn the shaft. I took the belts off in order to run the engine and charge the batteries without the propeller turning.

Jennie volunteered to clean up the grease in the engine room. She scraped, scrubbed and cleaned, and came out looking like a miner. She has been making lots of bits and pieces for the boat: cockpit rope holders – with slab reefing there's masses of cordage – a pencil container for the chart table as I spend half my time looking for pens, pencils and glasses. She has put up two pictures in the fore-cabin, a drawing of my granddaughter Bernadine, and a painting that Bernadine did of me fixing the boat.

We were just about to have breakfast when there was an almighty crash on the stern. The seas had been cresting and breaking for days and suddenly one hit the transom, came over the top, straight in through the main hatch and into the fore-cabin which was about four inches deep in water, ran back out of the pilot house, by the engine room and filled the bilge. There was water everywhere. The seats were soaked, and we spent the next couple of hours pumping out, mopping up, trying to dry things. Now the horse has bolted I've put a couple of boards in, but it may have been just a rogue wave which heaped up and hit us.

The ropes I fitted to the rudder wore through and so I've put and spliced thimbles in them with shackles to shackle them on. At present we are operating on two pulleys in the aft-cabin and what's left of the steering gear. I pull up one side or the other and then put a screwdriver into the rope like a Spanish windlass, put a twist in it to get the last quarter of an inch adjustment, with Jennie running backwards and forwards shouting out what course I'm on. This lasts from half an hour to three. The sooner I can get on with making, preparing and fitting the new quadrant the better. First of all I need a calm day, before braving the ladder again.

DAY THIRTY-ONE: 21 NOVEMBER 1986

Our position is 34° 58′S 48° 42′E. We gradually dried out over the last few days and I managed to contact Leon and tell him what was going on. We saw a bulk carrier, the first large ship since we left. Jennie spotted her and was so excited as she hadn't seen one at sea before. On the radio I discovered that she was a Filipino ship, the *Moya Lily*. I had a good chat with the skipper who said they had been warned about navigational hazards as the BOC race was in progress. It's reassuring to know that ships are looking out for yachts. One sometimes feels small and invisible.

Down the ladder again in my wet gear to get the ropes shackled to the rudder. That done, I dived under to have a look at the propeller. The rope was wrapped six or seven times around the blades. I tried to cut them with a carving knife tied on to a piece of wood but failed because the knife kept bending and I couldn't get it underneath. The boat slammed down in the water and hit me. As I was handing the knife back to Jennie she pulled a barnacle out of my head. I went down again, got a loop off and came up for air gasping, for breath. I was standing on the ladder when the boat ducked down and took me under. I swallowed about a gallon of salt water and was coughing and spluttering so much I had a job getting back up again. Jennie said that she would try, and put on my wet suit and mask. It was a bit too much for her as she's unused to diving and the boat was lunging up and down. I will have to try again sometime when conditions are better, as we've got to get it off.

A few days later I took the steering quadrant off, as I can steer from the cockpit on the ropes. Jennie had a go at the wind charger which had broken off. She propped it up and lashed it to a piece of wood, then straightened two of the blades which were bent at right angles.

The weather is dull and overcast. Nothing much is happening, so Jennie made some bread. I have been working on the quadrant for three days now. I laid it out on a sheet of plywood, nailing around its edge to hold everything in place, then wedging it level. I mixed some epoxy, glued the five bits together and fitted them in between the nails. I cut two pieces of 2 × 2 inch angle iron and glued and clamped these over the main joints, which gave me a good strong structure to work on. I made plywood inserts to fit inside the quadrant and glued the bottom one in place, making the internal part a good compressible structure. Glueing spacers on top of the ply to take the next sheet, I let the glue go off. The next stage was to fibreglass the inside of the quadrant and push in the second piece of plywood. I now had a box section fibreglassed on both sides of the quadrant, drilled four holes in the angle iron, threaded the holes and put in bolts for reinforcement.

We were going along at about 2 knots on a wet and overcast afternoon when the wind came up suddenly from the south. I changed course and put three reefs in the main as we were moving too fast. I took down the main and it blew force eight from nothing in twenty minutes. We are screaming along in big seas after almost flat water. Incredible.

In the middle of the night there was an almighty crash and the sound of something vibrating and rattling. I was pretty sure that the two bent blades had flown off the wind charger. I slid down the aft-deck, wearing only my harness, got absolutely soaked and tied up the rest of the blades to stop the wind generator shaking itself to pieces.

It gets light very early in the morning, at about half-past one. We are still on GMT and operating watches according to light and dark.

DAY THIRTY-TWO

The quadrant was ready so I welded the eye bolts for the cables using the Auto Arc Alternator, a high-frequency DC welder which makes a high-pitched buzzing noise. It worked beautifully. The only problem was that the boat lurched so much it was difficult to keep a steady arc.

I checked the engine oil which seems to be clean and not increasing in quantity, so maybe the diesel problem is solved. I disconnected the log which was playing up. The mileage was showing but not the speed.

Light winds from the east or south-east, difficult to make a good course. We are under full sail, tacking upwind in light air. This means frequent dashes out to winch up the ropes on the rudder in an attempt to keep her on course. After thirty days of almost non-existent steering, I have fitted the quadrant back on to the rudder stock and assembled it. It works beautifully. Without that, it wouldn't have been possible to tack upwind.

DAY THIRTY-FOUR

We have made little progress over the last three days, pinching courses, trying to get east and all the time going a little south of south-east or north of north-east.

Jennie was on the aft-deck fishing when a young albatross took her bait and got towed along behind the boat. We pulled him aboard and Jennie held down his wings while I grabbed his neck and managed to get the hook out of his beak. We freed him straight away and don't think he's suffered any ill-effects.

DAY THIRTY-SEVEN: 08.38 HOURS

After two days becalmed the wind came back and strengthened. I heard a horrible creaking sound from the foot of the mast. I thought it was the gooseneck but the mast was moving slightly in the tabernacle and our speed was going up. I decided to put one reef in the main and take some off the headsails. This did nothing to alter the speed but the course improved and she felt more comfortable. We went along like this all day and over the past four hours we've been knocking along at about 6 knots.

There seemed no point in the log being under guarantee in mid-ocean, so I took it to pieces. It's like a mini-computer inside. Leading from the switches are six wires painted on plastic which have only to be touched to send a pulse to a terminal. These had been badly folded when assembled and a couple of the wires were broken. I short-circuited the terminals with a screwdriver and in the end got it to work.

Our position today was 35° 21'S 55° 24'E and if this keeps up we'll soon be knocking a few degrees off. Had a QSO with Leon this morning. Someone in Australia has asked for news of me and Leon told them our position and news. The guy asked him to confirm that I was going into Albany. It's good to have friends looking out before we arrive.

DAY FORTY

A fantastic run! During the last twenty-four hours we have done 140 miles on the chart and come up to the sixtieth parallel of longitude quite quickly, with good strong winds ranging from force seven down to three. We could smell whales, like the smell of seaweed on the wind, but couldn't see anything. We've run out of wine and Scotch but Jennie has gone off the beer which makes me happy as we haven't all that much left. Strong winds and rain from the north after nightfall, and Jennie found a bottle of Scotch.

We've been listening in to the Durban maritime mobile radio network run by Alistair Campbell who is covering the BOC race. He gives the positions of the boats and weather forecasts for the area we're in, so we know where the high and low pressures are and when the fronts are coming through. I haven't contacted him yet as he is pretty busy with the race; I just listen in.

DAY FORTY-TWO

Becalmed again. I checked the solar panels to make sure they were working and found they weren't. I took them both off and could see that the positive wires had corroded underneath the mastic sealer. I repaired them; they are back, bedded in mastic, and working. I did some carpentry, boxing in the engine room and the passageway to the aft-cabin. Jennie fished with the rods unsuccessfully.

DAY FORTY-FOUR: 4 DECEMBER

It was calm enough early in the morning to think about attacking the rope again, still tangled round the propeller. At least it was calm before the wind picked up, which it usually does when I start a job. I went down the ladder with a big freezer knife and had another go but got nowhere. I then tried with a small penknife and managed to cut some off, still leaving rather a lot tangled around the blades. Diving again I tried to cut some of this away but was unable to get enough leverage or hold my breath long enough. I had to come up and rest, standing on the ladder up to my neck in rather rough water. Jennie suggested scissors and lowered them to me tied on to a piece of string. I went down again, this time fairly successfully but came up gasping for air and really fighting for breath. On the next attempt I got stuck between the ladder and the propeller and couldn't get out. I remember the panic as I struggled to get my head above water – my chest felt as though it would burst. I went down again, caught hold of the remaining rope, and that was that: the propeller was free at last and after forty-four days I could use the engine. I rested in the cockpit and tried to get warm, the water had been very cold. We had the last of the Scotch.

Listening in to the Durban net, I heard that Harry Mitchell on *Double Cross*, the English competitor in the BOC race, had had an accident in severe weather conditions, breaking a rib, hitting his head and was fast losing consciousness. The Durban net couldn't hear him but I could and relayed his position to Alistair Campbell for the doctor who was standing by. Harry was about 8° south-east of us and now that we had the propeller cleared we could motor to him if needed.

Early one morning, having finished the carpentry in the passageway and made the doors for the engine room, I thought I'd have a go at the galley while Jennie was still asleep. I got out the timber, hung the door, fitted the front on the cupboard, then took the gas cooker off its gimbels and repaired it. It had been shaken so much in the storms that all the nuts and bolts were falling out of the back. I repositioned the cooker and then when Jennie got up she sandpapered the woodwork and varnished it. We worked all day and the galley looks great.

The wind came back and we picked up speed. I corrected the course and she's doing about 5 knots on a lovely calm sea. Jennie is enjoying the hot sunshine, clear skies and beautiful sailing after those rough, cold, gloomy days. She thought she wasn't going to get any of this. She thought it was a pipe dream.

DAY FORTY-SEVEN

This morning I relayed messages about a French yacht, *Escoyen*, which capsized twice last night, losing the antenna. The mast is alright but the steering gear and wheel were lost, owing to winds of 65 knots.

DAY FORTY-NINE: 9 DECEMBER 1986

We're bombing along, terrific stuff, absolutely bloody terrific. In thirty-six hours we've averaged over 7 knots and in the last twenty-four have done 158 miles on the chart. We started quite slowly under full sail, the wind has gone round from the north to the north-west and we are right on top of a cold front.

Zane Spray is now far more powerful than she used to be. I couldn't have done such a large run with the other mainsail. The last twenty-four hours have opened my eyes, she's a dream. Just give her the wind and the right amount of sail and she's off. Full main, full staysail and half the jib. I can only use half because the halyard's broken and the jib would slide down the track if let out any more. The day's run on the chart looks phenomenal. The chart is folded over and we are more than half way. Australia is in the corner. We've something to aim for now and it's all downhill.

DAY FIFTY-EIGHT

The position today at 10.00 hours was 35° 53′S 90° 68′E. More trouble with the solar panels which cut out when hot but work again if a bucket of water is thrown over them. I discovered this today when waves were splashing and keeping their surface cool. We have had seas coming from all directions, enormous crashing waves. I would have liked to film them, but am worried about getting the camera wet. One day I'll stick it in a plastic bag.

Making good progress now. This passage could have been cut in half without the problems of the steering quadrant and propeller. We would have taken advantage of the engine while becalmed. For the first three weeks I was unable to use the mainsail as, with it up, I couldn't control the steering.

I spilled coffee over the log, charts and chart table. I put the cup down when speaking on the radio; the boat lurched and soaked everything.

DAY SIXTY

Bad news. The skipper of *Escoyen* is missing overboard and the search has been called off. His boat was found 100 miles south of Sydney and towed in two days ago.

DAY SIXTY-ONE

We sighted our second ship and tried to chat on the VHF. He didn't speak much English and didn't want to talk. He sounded Chinese.

DAY SIXTY-TWO

We spent the whole night becalmed. I hate the boat slopping around, so put on the navigation lights and didn't keep watch. The wind came back in the morning until it was blowing about force five. At this point the shackle on the main halyard block broke and the main slid down the track. I pulled it down and took the topping lift off the boom and on to the main to get it back up. I'm a bit short of shackles, halyards and blocks up there, but it worked.

We're putting local time forward now and have three watches going. Mine is at South African time so that I can keep tabs on the radio, Jennie's is at local time and the third at GMT. At 01.29 GMT, local time is 07.29 hours: a bit confusing.

DAY SIXTY-THREE

My longest time at sea and a fantastic first ocean crossing for Jennie. We'll be another ten to fourteen days before reaching Albany. Our last position was 35° 10′S 97° 58′E.

The wind has gone very light again this morning but we've had some good sailing over the last couple of days. The sails are slatting with not enough wind to hold them firm. We are looking forward to getting ashore after a cold, damp crossing with very little sunshine, only three or four days out of sixty-three. It's going to be pretty hot when we get in. Quite a contrast. It will be nice to meet some of the people I've been talking to on the radio and then go on to Sydney. I will have achieved half the world.

DAY SIXTY-EIGHT: 28 DECEMBER 1986

On Christmas Day (my second at sea – the first was with Chris Rudd on the Equator) we had greetings from Alistair on the Durban net and radio friends in South Africa and Australia. A contact in Cape Town rang Jennie's mother and gave her a message while we were on the air. It was quite a Christmas. Jennie had hidden a bottle of Scotch to give me. She made lovely decorations, most of them cut out of empty wine bags and cardboard. I didn't do anything while she did the cooking and made a Christmas pudding out of cake and mince pies. It was a relaxing day sailing very slowly with just enough wind to fill the sails. On Boxing Day we were becalmed again and I made some use of the time finishing the steps in the aft-cabin and putting a floor in the engine room. Life will be much easier when working on that side. I fitted folding doors to the sail locker on the other side of the engine, which is now sealed off in its own cabin. One day I'll soundproof it.

DAY SEVENTY-TWO

This is becoming quite a long voyage. We swopped watch at midnight and saw the New Year in by hurricane lamp.

DAY SEVENTY-SEVEN

Our approach was good with wind from the south until suddenly it went round to the south-east and up to gale force. We were being driven too far north towards land and I had to tack south and slightly west. On the second day the seas became rather steep, making it impossible to keep a good course. The wind went round to the east and we had to go either north-east or south-east. To give myself a little more sea-room, I plumbed for south, hoping the wind would change again.

DAY SEVENTY-NINE

Arthur Oliver, who runs the Travellers' net in Perth, has been giving me local weather reports. During the gale he said we would have south-westerlies today. I thought that was crazy. If you're going to get a front coming through it starts from the north and goes round. We were drifting becalmed most of yesterday and – Eureka! – the wind came up from the south-west and I had to run straight downwind. I tried goosewinging but the wind wasn't strong enough, the sails were flapping and she was going off course. This continued for about four hours. We were playing cards, a lethal game of Racing Demon, when I noticed that the sails were backed. The wind had gone round to the north. I handed the sails and set her on a new course.

We stayed up and we continued our game as the wind came up and settled. By first watch we were making good headway and have been ever since. If this only continues, we could be in Albany tomorrow.

I made the boat ready to go in and put up the courtesy flag. Getting out the fenders I blew these up using the bottle of CO_2 gas. I put the warps ready on the aft-cabin floor and ran the engine for an hour and a half to boost the batteries before putting the belts on. I checked the propeller and tried to put it into forward drive but the lever in the cockpit had seized solid. I sprayed it with WD40 but still couldn't get it to move. I went down below to look while Jennie tried turning the wheel, and heard the most awful crunching sound of gears breaking in the control box. All I could do was take off the control mechanism and turn it by hand. Getting forward drive on the propeller I started the engine, which promptly stopped with an airlock. I spent a frustrating day bleeding the engine, got it going and motored for a while. I now have forward drive but no reverse.

I started the Mase to boost the batteries. It misfired with a fuel blockage and without thinking I revved it up to try and clear it. This overloaded the generator: there was a cloud of smoke and smell of burning rubber as it burnt out. Thank God I hadn't made such a stupid mistake earlier in the passage.

When the gale hit us I had been toying with the idea of running up to Perth. It was 200 miles to Perth and 200 to Albany. I was right on the corner and could have gone either way. I'm quite happy with my choice because the wind has gone round to the north now.

DAY EIGHTY-ONE

Early in the morning we were scanning the misty horizon when Jennie cried out, having seen land again after the best part of three months at sea. A thin outline above the horizon. As we came in closer we saw it was solid and not a mirage. Trying the VHF I was surprised when the Australian Customs came back asking how many there were on board and what had been our last port of call. I gave them the answer and our estimated time of arrival at Albany. As we made our approach, running downwind close along under the towering cliffs, we met a three-masted schooner *Aquarius*. Carrying 11,000 square feet of sail, she was hard on the wind and tacked to go astern as she went by. I spoke to the first mate, who said that by the look of all the grass around my water line I had been at sea for quite a while. If we made it to Perth for the America's Cup we should come and see them.

Once I turned the corner into King George Sound the water became clear and blue, the white sandy beaches were glistening in the late afternoon sun and we could smell the richness of the land. In the distance we could see a power boat leaving the harbour and heading towards us. It hove to alongside and someone shouted that they were customs, come to escort us into harbour. The wind was so light and they were having difficulty going as slow as my 1.5 knots, so I started the engine. Outside the harbour entrance there was another airlock and it stopped; the customs boat threw me a line, towed us in and alongside the jetty. Amongst the sightseers were men in blue overalls who took our ropes and made *Zane Spray* fast and safe. What a terrific welcome, I thought. I had never had service like that before!

7

The Great Australian Bight

I should have guessed. The nice men in blue overalls were customs officials and before I knew it the boat was swarming with them. They went through everything, all our personal things. The cameras were opened, charts and ship's logs read and lockers emptied. Every now and then one of them would ask, 'What's this in here?' and I'd reply, 'Salt' or 'Parsley'. It wasn't until they asked if either of us were users that I understood exactly what they were after. Because the crossing had taken so long they assumed that we had had plenty of time to call in at Bangkok and then creep into Albany rather than Perth, where most yachtsmen wanted to be for the Cup. At one in the morning we were told that the boat was clean, we could go ashore and were free to do as we wanted.

We didn't get up until ten and as I slid the main hatch back I was welcomed by six customs officers waiting on the jetty. The chief was dressed in a wet suit, mask and snorkel. I laughed when I saw him and said that if he wanted to search the bottom of the boat he could take a scraper and clean it at the same time. They searched until midday, told me once more that the boat was clear and if they'd thought I was carrying drugs they would have got sniffer dogs from Perth. At this point I began wondering if Jennie could be carrying something, and she thought the same about me. I remembered leaving the boat unattended for six weeks in Cape Town; perhaps something had been planted and the customs tipped off.

We went ashore and had a big thick juicy steak for lunch, washed down with cold Australian beer, and then walked around Albany in the hot summer sun.

I was visited by Graham Tompkins, who had a boat on the other side of the bay at the Princess Royal Sailing Club. He told me that a berth had been saved for us and he would help take the boat over in a couple of days when I was ready. He arranged a meeting with a friend of his who could get some work on the boat done.

The next morning we woke to the sound of heavy panting. I looked out and there they were, the dogs from Perth. The Australian crew of the steam yacht *Enia*, who had been watching with interest over the past two days, shouted abuse at the men and invited us over for coffee, to give the bastards a chance to find the stuff, as they put it. Ignoring the officials we went over and from an opulent hundred-year-old craft watched them search in vain.

With Graham's help we took *Zane Spray* three miles to the sailing club. This little voyage wasn't without its problems, as after clearing the quay the engine stopped yet again. Graham, in his broad West Australian accent, said to me coolly, 'Christ, man, Cook didn't have an engine', and we sailed slowly and at peace with the world towards my new berth.

The next morning I heard the strains of 'The Land of My Fathers' wafting across the waters of the marina from a large ketch bearing the flag of the Welsh Dragon. I answered with a full volume blast of the Treorchy Male Voice Choir. Before long I had a visit from Dilwyn Morgan on a twenty-year voluntary exile from Fishguard.

The facilities at the sailing club are excellent: showers, washing machines and television room. On my first visit to the bar a member asked me to come for tea that night. We were not sure what tea meant; should we eat first as it might be only tea and cakes? We were pleased that we hadn't eaten as we sat down to a large three-course meal. I told my host about my first voyage and meeting Jon Sanders, an Australian yachtsman making a double non-stop circumnavigation. We had met in the middle of the Atlantic, he was heading south and me north. When I got to this part of the story he stopped me, got out Jon's book and showed me a picture of *Zane* II and a chapter on our encounter at sea.

One night I went to a telephone box to make a local call and found that it was not taking any coins. I thought that I would try and ring

Gillian in Wales and after twenty minutes it had cost me the princely sum of twenty cents (10p). Next, a half-hour call to Madeleine in South Africa: sixty cents. Finally I dialled Ann's number in London and got her answering machine. I couldn't miss an opportunity like that and gave her all the news, filling her tape. The following morning I went back to make more calls, to find a long queue. The next day there was no one there but the telephone had been mended. I went back to the yacht club bar and said to the only other man there, what a shame it was that they had fixed the phone box down the road. He replied, 'Yes. I've just done that. I work for the telephone company!'

The sailing secretary of the club heard that we were having difficulty in hiring a car (because of the America's Cup there were none left) and told us that if we were prepared to buy a spare wheel, a jack and do a little work on it, he had an old Ford Falcon pickup truck that we could use for the drive to Perth.

Our first stop was in the lovely old town of Fremantle which had been repainted for the occasion, but it was so hot – 105° – and full of tourists, so the only part of the America's Cup I saw was on a colour television in a cool old-fashioned bar.

It took two weeks travelling north along the coast to spot our first kangaroo. We kept asking where they all were and were told that it was hard not to see one in the early morning or evening. And once we had, they seemed to pop up everywhere.

On our way back to Albany we drove to Margaret River, the surfer's mecca, and on to the wild coast of Cape Leeuwin on the extreme south-west. Then we cut back through the forests of giant trees, one of which has steps that go around it to the lookout at the top. Jennie climbed it and got a certificate to say that she'd done it with courage, dignity and decorum. They gave me one to say that I hadn't done it with courage, dignity and decorum.

I had ordered a frame to be made in tubing to fit to the transom, making it possible for me to stand on it when working on the self-steering gear at sea. I repaired the propeller control using the gearbox and handle from a car jack. The next job was to weld guttering on to the pilot-house roof, with drain holes to catch rainwater, and pipe it to the tank. I finished each side and Jennie followed with a gallon can of paint, her hair in a ponytail to keep it out of her eyes. As she bent down to paint under the new gutter her hair fell neatly into the tin. She stood up to stretch and paint flew everywhere.

The Sailing Club held fun races on Friday evenings. We would set forth to do battle on the calm waters across to Albany town, armed with crates of beer and wine. There were only two rules: when meeting another craft one automatically called for water, no matter who had the right of way, and on arriving back at the club one should not be entirely sober.

On Saturday 21 February 1987 Jennie and I set sail for Sydney accompanied by twelve of our new Aussie mates. They cast me off from the marina and I reversed out slowly, but had too much pitch on the propeller when putting her into forward gear and the side thrust sent us back into the next empty bay. The club rescue boat had been standing by to take off our extra crew and decided that it would be safer to tow me out before I sank the rest of their fleet. Clear of the jetty, my happy band raised sail for me, took farewell photographs, sailed with us in the warm morning sun and boarded the escorting boat back to the club.

We tacked our way through the narrows into King George Sound and it was getting dark by the time we reached the open sea. The wind was coming from the south-east and the best heading I could make was south, but by the morning the wind had gone to the north-east and we made a free course to cross the Great Australian Bight. In the evening the winds went light and during the night boxed the compass from all directions but the barometer was dropping and at dawn the wind was strong from the south.

Jennie had been given a fish lure by a gold-prospecting fisherman, having told him that on the passage from Africa she had caught only an albatross. He told her that she would be certain to catch tuna with his lure, and she did, a fifteen-pounder. We had an excellent fish supper on our third evening at sea.

For the next few days the wind was kind to us. We saw plenty of shipping and could hear but not contact a Dutch single-hander in the *Boris Bravo*. He was heading for Melbourne to pick up a crew to start the two-handed race to Osaka. He was getting good radio weather reports which was useful to us.

I had bought a new Mase generator in Perth, this time getting the silent model. The first time I used it at sea in damp conditions I got such bad electric shocks that rubber gloves were necessary to insulate myself.

After averaging over 130 miles a day we fell into light head winds

103

and tacked back and forth some 300 miles south of Kangaroo Island, where Jennie celebrated her birthday at sea. The glass started to drop before long, the wind came up from the north-west and for twelve hours we were goosewinged and poled out on the headsails. The glass went on dropping and a raging gale blew for twenty-four hours.

On day fifteen the force nine wind went into the south-west and heaped up horrendous seas. We could hear *Boris Bravo* ahead report that he was running at 6 knots under bare poles in a 60-knot south-west wind. We had the smallest amount of staysail out and were racing down mountainous seas, when another low pressure system overtook us and the wind changed violently into the north again. We spent the night hanging on to our berths as the force eleven wind screamed and howled in the spray-filled darkness.

The following morning the wind was in the south, the sky clear blue, and *Zane Spray* was racing down the clifflike walls of breaking water. I stood in the pilot house watching while waves rushed by and sometimes went over the top. Jennie was trying to cook breakfast when I yelled at her to hang on. I could see a rogue wave some forty feet high, a pyramid of water racing towards the starboard side. It hit with the noise of a steam-hammer and I was thrown on to the windows as the boat went over on her side. The mast was in the water. *Zane Spray* was pushed under and all went dark. I had two boards in but the water came in through the eighteen-inch gap with enormous force and didn't stop until hitting the bulkhead in the fore-cabin. When the boat righted itself and I had dug myself out from a pile of charts, books and the Mase which had landed in my lap, I found Jennie under a heap of saucepans, bedding and food. The wave had rushed back, through the pilot house for the second time, down the passage and into the aft-cabin.

The seas gradually went down as we sailed in favourable winds towards the Bass Straits. We spent hours clearing broken glass, drying out clothes, bedding and carpets, extracting knives and forks from the heads, and then found ourselves becalmed ten miles north of King Island on a moonless sea of glass. The contrasts are so great that sometimes you might be dreaming.

In the darkness of that night we sat motionless, a whale occasionally breaking the surface in the distance. We could hear and smell its breath and it got gradually closer until we thought it would run into us. Then we heard it breaking water but could see only the line of white foam reflected from the lights of the boat.

The next day the wind came back, light at first. Further into the Straits the barometer fell and we remembered hearing the BOC competitors talking of the need to treat the Bass Straits with the utmost respect. Like the Tasman Sea, it can be quite nasty. By evening we were in rough grey seas, running down before the steep waves, and ahead I sighted four ships in a row crossing my bow. I called one that looked like a car ferry and asked him if he had sight of Rodondo Island and could give me a bearing. As we were talking the outline of the island started to appear behind his ship. I gave it a wide berth as there are strong currents, and by midnight had changed course to the north-east to head between Rodondo and the next island. We could relax a little as, although we still had shipping to contend with, we had left behind the small unlit islands and rocks and had a clear passage until reaching the oil fields next morning.

It was a calm, sunny day and with a light south-east wind we sailed as close to the oil rigs as one is allowed to, within 500 yards. We were surprised to find that some of the towering structures seemed unmanned and even unfinished.

On the night of the twenty-first day, the wind finally disappeared. We had reached the middle of the shipping lanes some ten miles off Cape Howe. This was approximately 250 miles south of my halfway goal, Sydney Harbour, and ten days earlier than the date arranged with Bob Stokes and the rest of the HTV film crew.

Jennie woke me in the middle of the night as there was a ship on a collision course with us. I belted into the cockpit to see it bearing down on us at speed. We were becalmed and motionless. I tried to start the engine and failed and called them on the VHF but there was no reply. The ship came on relentlessly. I got out the searchlight and shone it at the white-painted bridge, now no more than 200 yards away, where I could see figures standing. At the last minute they changed course and passed our stern by thirty yards while we stood shaking with fear, hearing voices on the bridge above the throb of the engines.

In my panic I had left the VHF radio on and ten minutes later heard a supertanker saying that a ship was on a collision course with him. There was no reply. He called again and again until finally a voice said, 'This is HMAS Cook. We are heading towards you but are not on a collision course.' The captain of the other ship was not satisfied and, although it was his right of way, decided to change course as the situation was dangerous. I didn't get on the radio to the *Cook*. I was too angry.

The next day varied from light winds to nothing and when the wind came back it was from the north with the current against us. We were being pushed back gradually and away from land. I had only one choice, to sail east until outside the warm coastal current that flows from the north, as the square-rigged ships used to. Outside the current the water temperature drops and the floor of the boat feels cold. A lot of Australian racing yachts trail a thermometer in the water to know whether the current is for or against them.

We had to sail south and east for two days away from Sydney before again tacking against light winds to the north, a hundred miles off the coast of New South Wales. Then our luck changed with a wind that started light from the south.

DAY TWENTY-EIGHT: MY LOG ENTRY, 20 MARCH 1987

Strong gale from the south, three reefs in main, half staysail, screaming along, makes the current we have been fighting for the last few days look pale.

The gale took us to thirty miles off Wollongong, where I had decided to stop as I was two days early for Bob. He was due to arrive in Sydney, sixty miles to the north. The wind went light, the sea flattened, and with warm sun on our backs we sailed in, picking out landmarks on our approach. Making the last few miles always seems to take forever. I radioed the coastguard to say that I would like to anchor in the harbour and would use my engine to get us in before dark. We hadn't run it since Albany and, while adjusting the propeller pitch, it jammed in reverse. Back to the coastguard to say we might be a little late.

We were within five miles of land when we saw a Police Rescue launch approaching, who hailed us. They had been sent to tow us in as we were having engine problems. I knew if I refused the tow, our fair wind would desert us. It was getting late and I could see that cold glass of beer standing on a bar waiting for me, so I accepted the offer. I didn't feel too bad about it: Joshua Slocum was towed into quite a few ports. Within an hour we were tied up alongside a busy fishing-harbour wall. Weekend sightseers came to see us. Between us and the far side of the harbour there was a clean sandy beach packed with children swimming.

We went ashore to eat at an ex-serviceman's club. These are excellent in Australia. One can get a good meal and drinks at half the price of most bars. We left to return to the boat, enjoying the luxury of a taxi, and had the good fortune to find one owned by a tall Scotsman, Bill Somerville. Bill was so interested in my voyage that he wouldn't accept the fare and continued to be our unpaid chauffeur for the rest of our stay.

Reporters from five newspapers and the local TV station turned up on the quay the next morning, wanting news of the boat that had been, apparently so dramatically, rescued from the sea. They had been told that we were becalmed for a week and running short of food and had been plucked from danger in the nick of time by the rescue services. When told the truth they did a more sensible story and ten minutes on television news.

I put a new set of belts on the transmission and got the boat shipshape, thinking that the motor would be needed on the passage to Sydney. While working I would stop to talk, as more and more Welsh people turned up to welcome us. Wollongong has a large Welsh community who emigrated to find work in the coal mines and steel works. One of them, Ray Lewis, took us home to have a shower and meet his wife and daughters. He suggested that I should return to Wollongong and work there on the boat when the filming was finished in Sydney.

I rang Bob to find that we had mixed up the dates; I must leave that night, as they had been in Sydney for four days and had to leave in another four.

I was ready to cast off. A TV camera was on the quay filming the coastguard patrol boat speeding in and out of the harbour on a make-believe rescue. On the second take, it raced around the corner behind *Zane Spray* and went out of control, spinning around in two full circles and revving flat out, hit my boat square in the stern, bending the new frame and transom, and breaking the links on the Sailomat. A ship's surveyor standing on the quay offered to submit drawings and an insurance claim for me free of charge. The coastguard accepted full responsibility for the damage. I told them it was a bit thick, coming halfway round the world to find myself nearly sunk by them.

By the time I had made temporary repairs and cast off, it was late at night. Jennie pushed the bow off the wall, I let out the jib and we sailed out of the harbour. There was a very light wind from the south and it wasn't long before we were becalmed near a reef. We motored for ten minutes, started to lose speed, and to my horror found the new belts had flown off and had chewed themselves up. When we had been knocked down in the Bass Straits the engine had moved on its mountings and must have been out of line when I fitted the belts. Having no engine, we put up the cruising chute and managed to scrape past the reef. By morning we were only twenty miles to the north of Wollongong.

Bob had said that he would hire a launch to meet me and do some filming, sailing at sea. By midday the wind was strong, had gone to the north and I was having to tack my way up the coast. I got through to Sydney Coastal Radio Station who relayed a message to Bob that I was still twenty miles to the south of the Heads at Sydney Harbour. An hour later we spotted a white gin palace with twin flying bridges, and as it drew closer we could see Bob and the crew filming as they circled us. A beaming Maori face on board bellowed that his name was Black George and they were coming alongside for the crew to board *Zane Spray*. I held the boat hard on the wind as in rough seas they glided past, jumped aboard and threw on bags, cameras and sound equipment. The filming continued, we had a glass of Scotch, and the excitement of having almost reached my half-circumnavigation started to reach me. Reboarding was not so easy, all but one got over on the first two passes, the assistant cameraman hesitated and on the third try Black George grabbed him and pulled him clear. As the launch was pulling away a wave pushed into our side, bending our rails, and there were nasty sounds of crunching fibreglass from the other vessel.

I had told Bob that I wouldn't be coming through Sydney Heads until the morning and would make one long tack out clear of land, so that we could rest between watches and start the tack back in the early hours. Like all best laid plans it didn't work out. I got into an eddy of hot current which took us out further than I had wanted and when I changed course in the morning the wind failed, leaving us on a hot flat sea. As the batteries were well down I started the engine, still without belts, to find something wrong with the alternator. I got out the Mase and the pull-start cord broke off. I called the Coast Radio Station to ask them to let Bob know I would be late, could not charge the batteries and therefore might not be able to call again on the VHF.

By midday the wind came back lightly and I could just lay a course to Sydney Harbour Heads, but as dusk approached the current took us close in to Bondi Beach. It clouded over, the wind died, heavy rain fell and the sky was filled with forked lightning which was hitting the water as we gradually drifted towards the rocks. I called the Coast Radio Station, using the last of the battery power, to tell them of our plight and ask if they could get Bob to organize a tow. Half an hour later we heard the sound of powerful engines: the Harbour Police once again, but this time making a genuine rescue, homing in by the light of my torch. Jennie took the wheel and they threw us a line. By now I was so tired that I could hardly stand.

We went through the Heads and saw the lights of the skyscrapers and ferries plying up and down the harbour like fireflies in the night. I couldn't hold the tears back: it was a scene from a fairy-tale. Then under the bridge again, where I had last been all those years ago as a sixteen-year-old deck-boy in the Merchant Navy, and into the darkness of Lavender Bay where I could see the headlights of a car piercing the still-dark night.

The police nudged *Zane Spray* alongside the quay. Neil the cameraman jumped aboard and gave me a hug as though he hadn't seen me the day before. A cheer went up as Bob yelled out, 'You bloody well did it then, David.'

8

The Barrier Reef and Tasman Sea

The next few days were taken up with filming and interviews with HTV. Bob had brought me a video camera, a Sony 8 mm AM, to use on the return journey. The mooring at Lavender Bay couldn't have been better: a walk through the park to North Sydney or a ferry to take one a mile over the water to Circular Quay, not far from the city centre.

Jennie had been given an introduction to Joy Cook, who asked her to spend her last few days with her in Sydney before flying home to Cape Town. She happened to mention the alarming episode with the HMAS *Cook*, only to discover that Joy's brother was captain of the *Cook*. Subsequently I met him at a party and pulled his leg about the incident. He maintained that there had been no real danger of collision, but agreed that they should have let us know what they were doing. He asked if there was any way in which the Australian Navy could help me, and the following day a launch came alongside bearing four gallons of white paint, two of primer, various mechanical parts and two stokers to realign the engine and fit the new belts. From a local factor I had bought link belts of a new type which would, they assured me, transmit the power required. After I had fitted them Ray came for the weekend to sail with me to Wollongong. We cast off and pushed her out backwards from the jetty. I started the engine in forward, found that the belts were slipping and consequently had no drive. She drifted slowly between the boats in the bay. We quickly raised sail and coasted between the moored yachts and under the Harbour Bridge. The wind, which was very light, failed and she drifted back under the bridge and into a bay further upstream. The wind came back and I decided to sail to Birkenhead to look at the problem, which I suspected was the propeller, by taking her out of water with a travel hoist. On the way the wind went again. We drifted in to an island and had to push her off, and sailed through the middle of a dinghy race, much to the disgust of the competitors. By late evening, tired and thirsty, we dropped anchor, which took, to our great relief. The next bridge upstream would have been too low for *Zane Spray*'s mast.

Next morning we were towed into the dock, lifted out and placed on the hard. The boat yard at Birkenhead was very busy as the *Aquarius* had docked. I rang Fenner's to ask their advice about the belts, which could not cope with the power of the engine. They supplied me with two sets of their new power belts in exchange for the old ones. While the boat was out of the water I fitted a new gland to the prop-shaft, two new pitch-control gearboxes for the propeller control, anti-fouled the bottom and, thinking it was time to have a new colour on the hull, painted her bright spinnaker red.

As I finished the last coat, a middle-aged Australian, Brian McCarthy, stopped by the boat and told me he had just finished building a 33-foot *Spray*, and asked whether he and his girl friend could look around. They then invited me to see their boat. Brian had made a really good job of it, and I remarked on the excellence of his sign-writing and asked if I could commission him to repaint the name on *Zane Spray*. He told me that I would find him too expensive but he would do it for nothing. He did it beautifully, painting the name on both sides of the bow, 'Aberystwyth, Wales, UK' on the transom, and two lines along the edge of the poop deck. As they wanted sailing experience I suggested that they should crew for me to Wollongong. They were delighted with the suggestion. The following day we motored seven miles down river, under Sydney Harbour Bridge and out of the Heads into the open sea. We set full sail in a stiff easterly wind and put her on self-steering, Brian noting every detail as he hadn't yet had his boat trimmed to go as fast as mine. We pulled into harbour at Wollongong that evening after a bracing sail. A volunteer coastal patrolman was waiting on the quay to take the ropes and make me fast for the night. We went ashore in the last of the warm summer rain and my crew caught a late train home.

111

Next morning Ray came to help me anchor in the middle of the harbour and offered me the use of a caravan in his garden and his daughter's Volkswagen Beetle during my stay. On Sunday he and his wife Carol drove me seventy miles to the gliding club where he is an instructor. He asked me to take a flight with him. I had never been up before and found it an exciting sport, like sailing in the sky. Ray let me take the controls on my last flight but after I had stalled three times and gone into a nose dive he thought it time to take us back to land.

As the autumn months went by Ray and his friend John Murphy took various parts needing repair to their workplace at BHP Steel-works. I worked on the boat, painting the decks and making gratings for the cockpit floor and seats. John was keen to sail the 600 miles to Mooloolaba with me, and Ray asked if he could join me in the Barrier Reef for part of the southern winter. Most weekends, when not flying we would enter the Wollongong Yacht Club races, enjoying ourselves learning to sail together and usually coming last.

Two men turned up on the wharf one day and shouted that my old friend Gareth Griffiths had rung from Wales and asked them to deliver a bottle of Scotch. They worked for Fenner's, and years ago one of them had interviewed him when he applied for a job. On being asked why he thought he was suitable, Gareth replied, 'Well, I'm Welsh aren't I?'

John and I set sail on the first day of the winter. My plan was to keep a north-east course until a hundred miles off the coast, outside the strong coastal current, go north until opposite Mooloolaba and then head in. At a cracking pace from the start, we set the sails outside the harbour entrance in a force seven south-west wind. Six days later it was still blowing force six as we arrived at our destination, having covered 800 miles.

Mooloolaba was warm and tropical and has a long inland waterway. The palmed back gardens of the houses, mostly with their own jetties edged the water. I berthed *Zane Spray* in the yacht club marina where the facilities were excellent. John's wife drove up to spend a week's holiday with him and they showed me a lot of Queensland before leaving.

While waiting for Ray to arrive by bus, I sat in the sun and occasionally did the odd job around the boat. Some repairs were done to the sails locally and I ordered a 1,000-square-foot spinnaker made like the Welsh flag, with a green bottom, white top and red dragon in the middle. The new sail arrived and so did Ray, and we raised it for the first time in a light wind while moored in the marina. It looked great against the clear blue sky and caused a lot of interest.

We decided to head north, going outside the Great Sandy Straits and get as far as possible, as Ray's time was limited. We set sail in a good south-east wind which carried us up through the Capricorn Passage, between the Sandy Straits and the outer reef, and on to the reefed lagoon and the islet of Lady Musgrave. After two days non-stop sailing, the wind changed to the north-east on our approach and started to whip up a nasty sea. We could see yachts off the palm-ringed white sandy beach and could have anchored on a lee shore, waiting for low water until the reef was visible and we could get through the narrow entrance into the lagoon, where the water was flat and clear blue-green, but decided it would be safer to carry on north for twenty-four hours and head for another group of islands.

Ray dropped anchor as I motored close in under the steep cliffs on the north side of Middle Percy Island. We sat on deck in the hot evening sun drinking beer and talking to a Dutchman and his crew on the only other yacht in the anchorage.

In the morning we motored round to West Bay. As we approached the golden beach we could see a tree-house in an old gnarled tree at the right of an inlet to a mangrove-edged lagoon. The waters in the bay were clear and warm with many tropical fish, and six other yachts rode quietly at anchor.

We inflated the Avon dinghy, mounted the outboard engine and explored the lagoon. Inside we found two catamarans moored in the shallow water. We went ashore, picked up coconuts and drank the fresh milk, then sat in the sea to cool off. We discovered that if the tree-house is empty one can stay there indefinitely rent free. On the beach, behind rows of palms, we found an open-ended A-frame build-ing with a barbecue at the back and hammocks upstairs to use if staying ashore. It is a local tradition that visiting yachts should leave something behind as a gift for the enjoyment of future explorers. Under one of the palms was a fresh water shower.

Percy Island is owned by Andy Martin, an Englishman who has lived there for twenty-four years as a hermit farmer, keeping sheep, goats, cows, horses and bees. The only way to the island is by yacht or small boat, keeping it completely unspoilt. Andy goes seventy miles to Mackay, on the mainland, once a month to get supplies, and when yachts return they carry goods for him. He serves lunch at his house for a dollar, the equivalent of 50p, to anyone willing to walk two and a half miles up the rough track. Ray asked him to come down to the beach in his clapped-out Land Rover to pick me up as I am unable to walk that far. The next morning he drove us up the steep path he had cut through the dense tropical rain forest, in parts hardly wide enough for the steaming vehicle to get through. We had to stop often to add oil and water. The house was of the old-fashioned Australian type raised on stilts with a veranda on all four sides. We had a good lunch with some other yachtsmen, discovering Andy sold mead, home made from tropical fruit and honey. He mixes it to your liking and there is a great deal of tasting not only of yours but everyone else's. By the time we arrived back on the boat with our two flagons we were in quite a happy mood. That night we slept well. I had sweet dreams and Ray nightmares.

There were two young Australians on a neighbouring 20-foot boat both keen fishermen. One night they left a strong line and bait over the side and woke to find themselves being towed out to sea by a large shark. They cut the line free and sailed back to the bay.

After a few nights ashore we made sail to follow the sun and head further north to St Thomas Island, where we stopped in a reefed bay. We tried a new method of spear gun fishing. Ray rowed the dinghy and, wearing my snorkel and mask, I would lie with my head over the half-inflated bow. With my left hand I indicated in which direction he should row and in the right had the spear gun. The other, more serious swimmers, watched this method with disbelief. We were not particularly successful.

North again to the Whit Sunday Passage and on to Hamilton Island a resort where tourists fly in by the thousand, perhaps not our best choice. While we were there the *Aquarius* sailed in to pick up some guests and take them sailing for a month. It was good to see the crew again.

There was an ancient wooden sailing ship in the harbour with tattered rags of sail still fluttering on the yards and a few planks sprung above the water line. We rowed over to have a look. It was a shame to let such a stout old vessel get in such a state of disrepair. The following night we saw it towed out into the channel, set on fire, and sunk: the death of a film prop.

I met the owner of a fish and chip shop, known as John The Pom

He was twice as large as life, a red-faced chubby man, a real cockney. I mentioned that I had been in the Merchant Navy. He had also been to sea and seemed to be about my age. I asked him if he had been trained at the *Vindy Catterix* and discovered that he was there in 1948, shortly after me. We had many mutual acquaintances. The *Vindy* was an old three-master on a canal in Sharpness, near Bristol. It was quite a tough training.

We decided to head back against the winds to Percy Island, making it our only stop on the way to Mooloolaba some 600 miles to the south. It was time for Ray to return home. Tacking between the islands and the Barrier Reef proved to be exciting. We had to be constantly alert as the hazards were many. We motor-sailed on one tack and sailed south on the other. The belts started to slip and I changed them for the new, deciding to replace the rubber engine mounts for solid ones when back in port. I felt sure the engine vibration was affecting the tension.

On the approach to Mooloolaba we started the engine, hoping to get in before the yacht club bar closed. There was an almighty bang, and I found that the welds on the clutch plate had broken. It took me an hour to drill, tap, and bolt it together while Ray tacked to keep us off the shore. We then motored through the still darkness, in to the entrance of the harbour and up the waterway to the marina. Spotting an easy-to-enter berth near the end of the pontoon, we made fast, walked to the club, ordered food and sat with a drink in our hands. It was hard to believe that half an hour ago we had been out at sea.

The next day, after Ray had flown home, a couple called John and Sandy Latham leaned on the rails for a chat. John was building a wooden yacht and hoped to give up his milk round to sail it. They were interested in mine and invited me to meet some of their friends, one of whom had a 26-foot yacht and asked if I would help him bring it through the Sandy Straits to Mooloolaba. I jumped at the opportunity as Ray and I hadn't gone that way.

After working out the tides, we set off from Tin Can Bay the next day to head twenty miles north to the entrance of the Straits. We went out to sea, keeping the beacons on the shore in line to get us over the dangerous bar. This had to be done at the right state of the tide. We headed south, arriving back in Mooloolaba in the early hours of the next morning.

A crew member from a large yacht saw my Welsh flag and paid me a visit. He was the son of a neighbour, and gave me the sad news of Moc's death.

The work continued well. I built shelves under the chart table and made gratings for the transom platform. I fitted steps up to the spreaders on the mast, made solid engine mounts, put on new belts, realigned the engine and changed the oil and filters. My sails were repaired and the boat made shipshape for the long journey home. The sailmaker, skipper of an aluminium racing trimaran, the *Mooloolaba Fire Truck*, asked if I would like to go out on her. Thirteen of us set off on a Sunday race. Only three worked and the rest sat on the nets between the floats drinking beer and enjoying the sun as she skated along at 15 knots. Two hours later, the cry went up that we were out of beer. The skipper replied that it would be a new experience to take the boat in while sober. He hit the quay as we did so.

John proved a good friend, helping me with both shopping and getting parts for the boat. He gave me timber offcuts and milk, soft drinks and cheese at wholesale prices, for my voyage to the Falklands. He and Sandy invited me to stay for the last two days, knowing that I had a hard few months in store. They came to help me cast off and say goodbye. John followed in his dinghy until I reached the harbour entrance. As he waved and shouted *bon voyage* I could see on his face that he wanted to be in my place. It was 3 October 1987. I motor-sailed for two hours to clear the estuary of the Brisbane River. Gradually the wind came up stronger from the north-east. The customs wanted me to go up river to Brisbane, a main port of entry, to clear my papers, which would have meant motoring up-river on the tide. With heavy shipping and numerous sandbanks the chances of sailing were pretty remote. I would then have to choose a mooring, go into the centre of the city to find their offices, do the paperwork and wait for them to decide whether or not to come and clear the boat. It would take me three days to do that, motor out again and get under way. I decided instead to make for Lord Howe Island, 150 miles off my route but a little further south. I would spend a few days there and clear customs.

DAY ONE

I let the preventers off too quickly and got some nasty burns. The rope pulled through my hands before I could let go of it.

116

DAY TWO

Thunder and lightning, the wind going to the north-west from force two to five and the barometer dropping until by night it was gale force eight. During the afternoon a hot wind came up and I saw hundreds of butterflies flying ahead of the storm. It was extraordinary. There is no land between here and South America. If the wind changes they might be lucky and hit New Zealand.

I've been feeling very sick and am finding it hard to be on my own again. This usually happens.

DAY FOUR

I filmed the new spinnaker flying, and she sailed beautifully on it but wouldn't go quite in the right direction. In the end I had to take it down. I had quite a struggle as the wind came up strongly and she leapt from 4 to over 6 knots. It was beautiful to watch and I had the staysail poled out on the other side. It was the first time I had used the pole and unfortunately there was a gust of wind and it broke. I lost the end with the pulley that I had made in Mooloolaba. The boat is in pretty good order at the moment but the propeller is again giving trouble. Finding forward and reverse is difficult which is a bit of a worry in confined spaces. Marinas are the worst.

After covering 450 miles on day four I approached Lord Howe Island. Ray Lewis had left a magazine on board which gave me some idea of what it actually looks like. It is difficult to get an impression from charts. There was an article about a yacht in trouble that had radioed ahead and got the local pilot, Clive Wilson, to show him the way in through the reef. I tried to raise him on the VHF and the customs answered my call. I asked them if I could go straight in or did they normally send a pilot out. They told me to stand by while they found out. I waited, got back on to them and was told that they had been unable to get through to the island; I asked whom I was talking to. It was a coastguard station in New South Wales, over 400 miles away. As VHF has a normal range of about twenty miles, conditions must have been very strange. I was only two miles from the reef by the time I finally contacted Clive who came out to meet me. The entrance is quite dodgy as the island has a reef on the west side. You have to come through a gap with breaking seas on either side pounding away on the rocks. Clive helped me pick up the mooring and welcomed me in.

The islanders are descended from the crew of the *Bounty*, some of whom left Pitcairn and resettled here. They are quiet people and speak with a rather old-fashioned English accent, from the time of their ancestors.

Next morning a yacht, the *Vida*, came in from the Hacking River, near Sydney. The crew of seven invited me to join them at the local fish restaurant that night. They asked me about my voyage, and the man sitting next to me mentioned that he was with the River Police. He thought he knew me and it transpired that he was one of the two policemen who had towed me in to Sydney. Odd how these things happen in what seems to be the middle of nowhere. It reminds me of one of Tristan Jones's books. Some of the coincidences sounded a little far-fetched. But now I'm not so sure.

After a few days I set sail for the Bay of Islands, New Zealand, about 850 miles away, and did 140 miles in the first twenty-four hours. The barometer began to drop. I could still hear the mainland weather stations. Strong winds were forecast from the south with a front coming through.

DAY TWO

During the evening the wind came up to near gale force, followed by lots of rain. In the night I woke and thought something was amiss. I looked at the compass and found myself heading north: the wind had changed. Waiting until the rain stopped, I dressed and got her back on course before it started again. I was lucky to get this done in a dry period. We have been going like the clappers ever since and are still making a good course.

The rolling sea has been uncomfortable. I felt sick going to Lord Howe Island and on this part of the passage as well. I don't know whether or not I have a stomach bug but feel sick most of the time. Perhaps it will pass if I keep on taking Scotch.

I've made a terrible discovery. I opened the fridge to find that the gas had gone out and the food had thawed. Inside were a couple of rotting chops, an avocado and some tomatoes. What a smell! Maybe

118

this is why I've been feeling sick. It's now all clean and the food is over the side. Nice for the fish.

As it is risky putting the camera out on the stand in this weather I cover it with a plastic bag, leaving a hole for the lens, stand in the main hatch and switch it on. When the weather is kinder I'll film myself doing some work around the deck.

It's blowing a real hooley out there. I was asleep, and woke to hear a shrieking sound. How lovely to be safe at anchor, I thought in my half-conscious state, it would be terrible to be out at sea. The boat was being hurled about violently and I realized that I wasn't at anchor at all but screaming along at about 7 knots. I put a bit more weather helm on straight away to try and keep her downwind. I need to hold on to all the sail I've got. I hope it won't last too long, it's raining like hell out there. Pouring down.

This is the first time I've been so cold for ages, getting into southern latitudes again. The wind is coming up from the south and it's freezing.

I once heard Tristan Jones say, during a radio interview, that when he retires he will sling an anchor over his shoulder, land in Mexico and start walking inland. He will continue walking until someone asks him what he has got on his back. Then he'll throw the anchor down and stay, because if nobody knows what it is, they won't be able to talk boats. I feel like that.

This morning the auxiliary batteries were nearly flat, only a glimmer of light, so I must charge them today. I have had no navigation lights on for two nights but have used the radio and tape recorder. I must be a bit more careful when I leave New Zealand. If I can get off the beaten track and not have to worry about lights, maybe I won't use so much fuel charging the batteries. The Mase is in its new place neatly mounted in the sail locker on a platform, and the exhaust is now piped outside through a mushroom vent. This was one of the things I did in Mooloolaba. The engine is so quiet now that it's really quite acceptable.

Progress is still good. The wind has gone down considerably to about force four. The slower it comes up, the longer it will last, they say. I'm about 300 miles from the top point of New Zealand and trying to get around a bank on the sea floor. I don't want to go over it as it's ninety metres at the shallowest point which might well cause rough seas. There will almost certainly be fishing boats, another hazard to avoid. I have to read the charts of the ridges and sea mounts on the bottom as they affect the sea state. There has been a ship in front of me for a long time, heading north very slowly. It was either trawling or fishing, the first I've seen for ages. My position on Day Four is 32° 41'S 166° 47'E.

I have just taken a big sea over and there's water inside on the cushions which should teach me to keep the louvred doors shut. It was a big one which came out of nowhere, straight over the top of the boat, filling the cockpit. It was ages before it drained away and the gratings were floating. I'll tie them together, so that they don't drift away.

I am only about a hundred miles off North Cape now and this is only Day Five. It's half-past three in the morning at the moment, local time, exactly twelve hours ahead of the United Kingdom. It makes life easier, as when it's twelve o'clock at night I know it will be midday at home.

I have just heard a forecast on New Zealand Radio. The wind should change to the north in the next twenty-four hours, sending me straight down to the Bay of Islands. At present I'm making fair progress in the midst of a gale and attempting to cook a meal. The water keeps trying to get out of the pan, coming up in globules, staying stationary in mid-air and, sizzling hot, dropping on my foot.

It's been blowing hard all day. I'm very, very tired. I tried to sleep during the day, but couldn't. The crashing of the seas is horrific and the waves keep coming right over the top. I have been knocked down for the second time and my heart seems to stop. I was thrown on to the starboard windows and found myself looking down into deep green water until she righted herself again. I have to tell myself that only 200 miles away a tranquil bay is waiting. Twelve days ago I set off from mainland Australia. It was nice and warm in Mooloolaba and I'm missing that now.

DAY SIX: SATURDAY MORNING

A rough old night which got worse and worse. I reefed the main down, as she was not making a good course, and tried to slow down as I was going fast in the wrong direction. A fix will tell me how far north I was blown and how far east I've still to go. I'm still waiting for the wind to change. It seems to have gone round a bit this morning, but must abate first and come up from a new direction. There's not much

I can do against this. At the moment I seem to be heading away from my goal. It wouldn't be so bad if I were going straight to Cape Horn and could pick the best possible course. I need to go south-east and that's where the wind is coming from.

It was an unpleasant night, with a screaming wind and the sound of the boat crashing on the waves. It makes a hell of a noise. I tend to worry about the welding, but at least I know I've made her very strong. She would have broken up by now if not. I need this wind change. Every muscle in my body is sore with being chucked about and I've terrible diarrhoea. In fact I'm feeling pretty 'crook'. Oh well, it will get better.

I had a high-low (not very accurate), fix on the Sat. Nav. and I'm waiting for a better one. I switched on the radio, but listening in is impossible as the Sat. Nav. causes so much interference, a squealing sound. With the volume turned up I could just about hear news of a storm. I think I got the gist of it. There has been a hurricane in New Zealand, trees have been ripped up and cars blown over. If it was as bad as that I've been lucky.

DAY SEVEN: 17 OCTOBER 1987

My position of 33° 53′S 172° 36′E puts me approximately 35 miles north of New Zealand and about 120 miles from the Bay of Islands, if I could go in a straight line, that is. The wind is still heading me, coming from the south-east. I'm going south at the moment and when I get further down will have to put her on the other tack and try to make a degree or so to the east before another tack down. It's hard to take, after such a good run. It was a terrific six days and if the wind hadn't changed I'd have reached here twenty-four hours earlier. The prospect of getting in during the next couple of days doesn't look too brilliant. The weather is pretty average, the wind has gone down, but the seas in these parts just don't seem to go flat.

I'm so tired that my legs will hardly support me. I tend to put off doing things that I should, even eating, although I try to make sure that I have enough. My stomach upset is better but I haven't felt so weak before. I think an infection must have drained my strength and all the rough seas have brought me down. When I reach the Bay of Islands it should be warmer. It's not cold by home standards, but after the tropics it feels pretty nippy. The wind factor and damp make a lot of difference at sea. It's overcast now but was clear this morning.

There's a broken cord on the self-steering gear, which I should mend, but I'm hoping the seas will flatten out and make the job easier for me to carry out. It's not urgent but it should be done. I hope to get another fifteen miles or so nearer land and then I think I'll tack her.

I heard something splashing and had a look at the bilge. It's full again and I emptied it only yesterday afternoon. It isn't coming through the shaft and the only other place I can think of is the exhaust pipe which is at the bottom of a very full sail locker. I will have to take everything out and look and see what's happening.

It's a complete mystery – the exhaust pipe is dry. I shall have to pump out regularly now which doesn't bear thinking about. It's hard physical work and has to be done hourly. I hope it doesn't get any worse. I can't see where it's coming from, but a weld has probably gone on a seam and the water is trickling through. I'm going to sit down and enjoy a warm gin and think how nice it will be in the Bay of Islands. I can always slip the boat on to the hard to check it over, if necessary. We've taken quite a pounding in the last few days, so there may be a little split somewhere. Anyway, gin first.

'Land Ho!' at half-past three in the afternoon. I can see it! I can see quite a lot of it, but I'm not quite sure yet which bit I can see. I'll try to identify it shortly. Yet another country sailed to on the dreaded Tasman Sea, which has flattened down considerably, probably because I'm in the lee of the land. I may have to tack to the east once more. When I know where I am I shall decide what to do.

Eleven o'clock at night and I've had to charge the batteries. I've used a lot of power in the last twenty-four hours and the Sat. Nav. stops working when the voltage is low. I need it at present, and also the lights as I'm in a fair amount of shipping. I have been feeling so ill that instead of keeping watch until midnight, I've been putting the lights on, going to bed and sleeping. When I set sail again, once away from the coast, there shouldn't be so much shipping and I'll go back to sailing without lights, hoping for the best: a bit like Russian roulette.

The sea calmed as I got closer to land and not so much water leaked into the bilge. I'm beginning to wonder if it could be coming back through the bilge pump itself, the force of the waves pushing it back past the valves. If that's the case I'll have to fit a seacock and open it before pumping. I replaced the bit of cord on the Sailomat, not making a very good job of it, but at least it works. I've had to change course as I was coming down on the land. I thought I was going to miss North Cape by two miles, although I'd planned it carefully on the chart. I will have to put in a tack.

I saw a ship from the Isle of Man, *Ford Steel*, and had a nice chat with the skipper, asking him for weather information. He described his weather fax picture to me and told me that high pressure was over the North Cape at the moment. He thought it was moving over and going east, so it should be here in about twelve hours, with northerly winds, which will be terrific. While I was talking to him the boat gybed, tacked herself and stood there with her sails backed. I asked him to wait for a few minutes while I sorted things out, and while getting her on to a new course, caught my toe under a cleat. I think it's broken, as it's bent, blue and rather sore. I hobbled back to him and finished the conversation.

As I went away from land and, I hoped, the shipping lanes, I tried to sleep. The Bay of Islands is sixty miles to the east. I'm trying to get enough room to clear land, and hope that the wind then goes round to the north. At the moment I'm charging the batteries, waiting for it to finish as I don't want to go to sleep with the Mase running, in case of fumes. These smell very strong when the wind blows exhaust back through the hatch. I must decide whether I've gone far enough on this tack. I have to watch it because if the wind turns I could find myself going north-west again. Whatever the wind does, she follows on the self-steering.

DAY EIGHT: SUNDAY 18 OCTOBER 1987

It's actually the end of Day Eight and the beginning of Day Nine as I'm on Greenwich Mean Time and my day doesn't end for a little while yet. It has taken me all night to pass the North Cape. I took some rather wobbly film of it as I'm not feeling very steady. I put in a big tack during the night which took me far enough to the east to have another stab at getting south. The wind had changed and it wasn't as good as I thought it would be.

It's a grey day. I'm going to play it by ear now. I must spend another day and night at sea before either getting in at dawn tomorrow or having to shoot off somewhere to anchor. There are a couple of bays further down and I'll see what the wind is going to do before making a decision. If I stay at sea, I'll slow down about thirty miles from land, in order to arrive at daybreak just after five in the morning, at first light. That's the plan.

DAY TEN

The last twenty-four hours have been murder. I sailed down the coast of North Island on the strength of the weather fax prediction which was completely wrong. I was getting very tired, tacking against the wind, and got down to Cape Kerri Kerri, with about fifty miles still to go. I slept for short periods while tacking down the coast and woke to see lights on the shore. I was in too close and had to head out again. The wind altered the course slightly and I found myself going the wrong way. This continued for hours and at two o'clock I decided to motor away from land and down towards the Bay of Islands. I started the engine and everything went fine for a time. I couldn't sleep, was weak and very tired, but had to make sure I was still on course. At daybreak I realized I had still another forty miles to Opua.

Everything seemed to be going well until the engine stopped. I was really feeling too exhausted to try and sort things out, but had to. I bled the engine, restarted it and motored for half an hour, when it stopped again. I was closer in to land and in a dangerous position. I got the sails up, tacked out and once more bled the engine. When exactly the same thing happened again I checked the fuel system and cleaned the filters. There was quite a bit of dirt in one of them but I managed to get her going, this time successfully.

Meanwhile the wind was still heading me. I tried to sail, but the wind headed me. I got into the bay and the water went calm. It was warmer, the sea was blue and seemed to smell of the scent from the trees. It was so strong, like new-mown hay, and the air seemed to be full of it. It's a wonderful smell when you come in from the sea.

I got through to Kerri Kerri Radio and asked if they could make sure somebody was on the quay to catch my rope, as I was single-handed. Motoring the twenty miles to Opua I recognized the jetty from a photograph in the pilot book. There were crowds of boats but I could see a space at the far end of the quay. I went for it and one of the linkages broke as I used the propeller control. I had forced it and I hadn't any drive. Luckily I was coasting at about the right speed. I shouted over to the fellows on the quay, they caught the ropes, pulled me in and tied me up. It was a joy to be safe. I was in.

I told Des Renner, who works for the harbour board and was one of the men who helped me, that I was going to the Kerri Kerri Yacht Club, and he explained that there are moorings but no marina, the club opens only at weekends and is a couple of miles walk from town. I said that I have a bit of a disability, find walking any distance difficult and asked if I could stay on the jetty. Des agreed but told me there was a slight problem. A big race was coming up from Auckland that weekend and would I mind if some yachts tied up on the outside of *Zane Spray*. I didn't mind as my boat is made of steel, and in the early hours of the morning I heard an occasional bump. By the time I got up, about 150 vessels were surrounding me. Every five minutes feet marched over my deck and I was passed a beer. I met some of New Zealand's top yachtsmen and discussed my next leg with Peter Blake who had been round the Horn many times. Since the boats got in, gallons of booze have been drunk. It's going to be a hard weekend.

A man from the Ministry of Agriculture and Fisheries came to inspect my stores and, as in Australia, confiscated all the fresh vegetables, fruit, pasta, honey, popcorn, eggs and cheese. I asked him why, and was told it was to protect the farming industry against imported crop diseases. It was all to be incinerated on the jetty. At the end of the week a dustcart took foodstuffs from the skip to a nearby open tip to be eaten by birds.

A Welsh boy turned up who has been living there for several months. He works as a boat builder in Whagarei not far away and said that I could go in to work with him, borrow his car for the day and see a bit of the country. He invited me for a meal one night and so did Des.

Every morning I saw a wiry old woman rowing a heavy wooden dinghy ashore from a large ketch anchored in the bay. She used to stop and talk to me. It wasn't until I recognized the name on her boat, *Wanderer* V, that I realized that she was the legendary Susan Hiscock.

A car ferry runs from here to the other side of the Bay, and the Maori skipper shouted over to me asking whether I could give him a Welsh dragon flag for the ferry. I hadn't got one but did have an Aberaeron Yacht Club burgee. I took it over this morning and he invited me for coffee on the bridge while he took the ferry across to the other side. It was designed in Britain, having two propellers on opposite corners, one forward, one aft, and can be revolved around in

360°. He showed me how to work it, and in the middle of the bay spun it around in a couple of circles to prove how manoeuvrable it was, full of cars and passengers.

A lot of boats sail in at this time of year to shelter from the summer cyclone season to the north. Ray Martin, from the west coast of Canada who usually sailed single-handed, helped me on the boat, and on the day I was to leave went up to check the mast and the rigging. Before he and other friends cast me off, I gave him the video camera to film my departure. He followed in his dinghy and sailed with me a little way down the bay, handing the camera back before returning. Once more I was at sea.

9

Double Black Friday

On 11 November 1987 I left the Bay of Islands, having made a commitment to myself to make for Stanley via Cape Horn. I felt good about it. I motored out for three hours with the main, getting a bit of lift from the wind which started to pick up as I got near Cape Brett. The log was not working and was covered in barnacles which I cleaned off from within the boat. I saw an incredible sight: a windmill on a catamaran, sailing straight upwind with a three-bladed propeller on the mast. I had heard of someone in New Zealand who had built one, so perhaps this is Mark Two. It seemed to be working well.

DAY ONE

The wind has gone pretty light and I'm doing between 2 and 3 knots. The sky is clear, it's hot and the sea is tranquil. The wind could be a little stronger, but one can't have everything. At least I'm off. I have forty-five days to get to Cape Horn if I'm going to make it by Christmas, then another week or so on to Stanley. That's if I average 120 miles a day. Once in the roaring forties I should have a bit of a lift from the current as well, maybe from a half to one knot. I need to average 4 knots which shouldn't be too difficult with decent winds from the right direction. I hope to film some icebergs during the month.

127

DAY TWO

Very slow stuff. Last night I was barely moving, slatting sails, doing about 2 knots, and at daybreak the wind went altogether. I sat until lunchtime when the wind came up gradually and my speed went from 2 knots to about 5, on a good course. I'm trying to miss an active volcano under water, the Rumble Seamount, about 100 metres under the surface. If it erupts it could make a bit of a splash. I shall give it a reasonably wide berth. My last fix was 177° 26′E, not all that far to 180°, the date line, opposite Greenwich.

I'm halfway around the world, and from now on start going downhill again, from 180°, 170° to 150°, and west not east. I either gain a day or lose one when I go over the date line. It makes my mind boggle but this morning I found a good description of it in Reed's, a nautical almanac. When I get to the date line I'll read it again and decide which day I'm in. It could be very important to my navigation. A lot of people have calculated it the wrong way, and when looking for an island in the Pacific have missed it by hundreds of miles, running into reefs that they didn't think existed.

A fishing boat came visiting yesterday evening. I was enjoying a rum and Coke and saw a large shape outside. I dashed out to see a boat on a collision course, 200 yards away and heading straight for my beam. I could see the crew waving from the bridge and as they pulled alongside the skipper shouted, 'Where are you going?' I got out the loud hailer and bellowed, 'The Falklands via Cape Horn.' 'Good on yer, mate,' he replied. They were tuna fishing and had seen me from miles away on the radar, recognized a sailing boat and came to say hello.

Last night I managed to make contact with Des in Opua. We had a quick chat and I could hear Paul on the frequency as well. tried to call him but he couldn't hear me. He wasn't expecting me the breaks in his transmission were very short and somebody else cut in.

There's a good wind now, about force five from the north-east, and I'm screaming along in the right direction. The local radio forecast for Auckland was that 20-knot winds and rain were coming, after which the wind would go round to the south-west, rain again on Sunday and then clearing up. It looks as though I shall have a bit of a push. It's always nice to make a good start. The first day wasn't bad, I did about 95 miles from Opua but I need a few days at 140 to get my average back.

FRIDAY 13 NOVEMBER: 36° 01′S 177° 54′E

I've done 126 miles in the last twenty-four hours. My speed's been going up the whole morning and there is a strong wind warning out for the Auckland area, now 200 miles away, for winds of 30 to 35 knots. Gales under way. I shall use as much of the wind as I can and tonight I shall reef down and slow her a bit as I don't want to be caught out in the middle of the night.

It is only about forty miles to the international date line and I'll have an extra day as I go across. This gives me a day more than I'd thought in my calculations to get to the Cape by Christmas. I shall cross it today and have two Friday the thirteenths, one after the other.

NEARING THE END OF MY SECOND FRIDAY THE THIRTEENTH

At dawn there was a thick fog, a real pea-souper, but hot and muggy. I'd put my position down on the chart, finding I'd travelled 150 miles in the past twenty hours. I'd thought it would be a record run but the wind died completely. I had hoped for more.

I was pretty ill during the night. I'd eaten a meat pie which didn't do me much good, and the motion of the boat was horrific.

Visibility has been bad with rain and fog. I seem to be going south-east, straight towards the ice; maybe it has a magnetic attraction for me? There's just a breath of wind now and she's up to 2 knots. I hope it'll settle in for a while. I'm making great strides on the large-scale chart which goes halfway across the Southern Ocean. The next has Cape Horn in the right-hand corner and nothing but ocean in between. It will encourage me to get to the point where they join.

THE AFTERNOON OF 14 NOVEMBER

I shall catch up on a bit of sleep. I'm still feeling pretty washed out and haven't been sleeping. I'm hoping for a bit of wind. Only the main is out now as I took in the headsails, which were wearing themselves out. The main acts as a brake to the rolling; if I took it down, the boat would gyrate all over the place. I'm not moving, just pointing in the right direction.

The wind came up eventually from the south-south-east and I'm off again. I must have been sitting slap in the middle of two systems. The sails were slatting first north, then south, north and south, carrying on like that all day, but at last I'm away in a bit of a gale. From nothing four hours ago to pouring rain, taking seas over the top, reefed right down again. I look rather odd. Not wanting to get my tracksuit trousers wet, I put on only the top of my heavy weather gear and am running around with a bare bum. It's not too cold and it's easier to dry off and put on my warm trousers afterwards. Otherwise I've got to change everything, which is cumbersome and takes so long. I'm now going north of east, whereas before I was on a nice course to the south-east and had been since leaving. I want to lose some of that south. I've sailed far enough not to worry about a little detour as long as it's more or less in the right direction. It's a grotty old night, black as pitch. I'll try and get some sleep.

DAY FIVE

Only thirty miles from lunchtime yesterday till dawn today. The little wind there was went, and I spent four hours sitting, waiting for the wind. Now it has picked up from the east, but so light that all I can make is north or south, and I've turned south, hoping to have a little help from the current. Thick fog again, miserable. Saw a little chink of blue this morning and then it closed in. I'm in a cocoon of fog, like being in an opaque goldfish bowl.

Last night I got Paul on the radio. He found difficulty in copying me but I could hear him. I managed to get through to his mate in New Zealand who relayed everything to him. Now that they know my frequency they will be listening for me. I also contacted the ANZA net, (Australia, New Zealand, Africa) who relayed to Leon. I'm 500 miles off the coast of New Zealand and have worldwide contact, which is satisfying.

I charged the batteries last night with the Mase. The solar panels are giving out about 1 amp, which isn't bad as it's foggy and early morning. I shall sit here and contemplate my miserable lot, wishing the wind would come up from an easier direction. I've been at sea for five days and am not yet settled in. It's not a good time: midway

130

between a short voyage and a long one. Limbo. And my average is down to 100 miles a day.

DAY SIX

I sat here until evening when the wind came back from a good direction, allowing me to sail south-east. I started to reef down just as it was getting dark, and the best course I could make was south. At least I was moving. It was pretty uncomfortable as there were big swells from the south and I was plunging straight into them. I stayed up until midnight and kept reefing down until it was up to a full gale, with three reefs in the main and about a third of the staysail out. She was going along pretty fast.

I put on the lights and went to bed for four hours, getting up a couple of times to check everything. This morning I was making a cup of coffee when I saw a two-inch round hole at the foot of the staysail, looking as though something had gone right through it. I can't imagine why a hole should appear there. It's not a tear, which could happen easily. I nipped out smartly and furled it in a couple more turns so that the hole was wrapped around the stay. I shan't be able to use more of that sail until I get a chance to repair it.

Well, I had a good start. Two Friday the thirteenths, becalmed for two days and then, on top of that, a gale. The wind is coming from the east, which is most unusual here. It's mostly west, north, north-west, south or south-west, but rarely east. During the night the wind-generator lost the vane which holds it straight into the wind. It's still going round at the moment because the wind is strong, but I shall have to sort it out.

DAY EIGHT

Hell! Another problem. The forestay bottle-screw has broken and the stay is hanging on by the strap that stops it from turning. It's a real bugger and I don't know what to do. There's not much I can do at the moment because the gale is tossing me around all over the place. I got it fairly tight by sheeting the sail in, stopping any movement in the stay. I was worried that this would break the strap. I shall pray for fine weather so that I can get out to repair it. At the moment it would be plain bloody dangerous to work on deck, and the mast might come down if I tried to do anything. I need calm weather. Once I release the forestay, the top of the mast will no longer be supported, could work itself backwards and forwards and break off at the spreaders. I must find some fair weather and lash everything down to take the strain off the mast: a major operation. I'm in trouble. I've a spare sail which I could use if the worst comes to the worst but it's not as good as the one that's on. All is not yet lost but it looks and feels like it. I'll have a Scotch and consider the things that are going right. The amp meter is showing 2.5 from the bit of light coming through the clouds. I'm trying to cheer myself up....

After a Scotch, I worked out another plan which could be used in the right conditions. I could make up a block and tackle to tension the stay, using ropes rather than a bottle-screw. I've only about six inches to work in, and it would depend on how much give there is in the ropes. I could get extra tension by lashing the stay to the forerail, make a Spanish windlass with a few loops of rope, and put in a piece of wood to twist around which will tension it like a bottle-screw. It wouldn't be necessary then to take everything apart and risk losing the top of the mast. That's the biggest problem: the prospect of losing the mast. The same thing happened on *Zane* II. I was about halfway across the Southern Ocean when the bottom half of the bottle-screw broke, but on that occasion I had a spare stay fixed to the top of the mast. This time I was cutter-rigged, having two stays up at the front of the mast, and didn't think I'd need a spare. I was wrong.

If the right weather doesn't arrive, there are four places which I could try to reach: Gisborne, Napier or, if the wind takes me south and west, Christchurch, and if that fails, Chatham Island. According to the pilot book, none of them are particularly easy to get into and if the storm continues I might take the decision to run with it and go back to New Zealand. If I do that it will be difficult to work up enough enthusiasm to leave again. Maybe I'll feel better after a rest. I should be able to repair it, and if I were another thousand miles out, there'd be no point in trying to return. Up until now I've managed to mend everything necessary at sea and with a little help from above and better conditions I might manage it this time. It's not plain sailing. It's bloody well not.

DAY NINE

I made a temporary repair by lashing down the stay. I used a hook threaded through a chain, and shackled it down. I'm now about 250 miles to the north of Chatham Island and have decided to go in there for repairs. I should be able to get the bottle-screw welded. Maybe I'll do the inner stay as well, just to make sure. Another problem is the staysail. I've discovered two more tears on the foot and dare not put any more of it out. I'm doing about 4 knots on not a bad course. Two or three more days like this and I might reach harbour. That's my plan. I must have hope. I'll have something to eat – tomatoes on the last bit of bread, perhaps. I haven't felt like making bread. Things would have to be more settled and warmer. I'll have a bit of a rest....

It's 58°F now and I'm 40°20'S, the furthest south I've been. Chatham Island is about 45°S. From there I'll be in a good position to take the shortest route across to Cape Horn, leaving on a good wind in order to do the first few hundred miles quickly. That would be nice. I will be there for several days for repairs and drying out the boat. It needs it: everything is damp and cold.

DAY TEN

I raised a ham operator on Chatham who gave me instructions on getting into Waitangi and warned me of local dangers. He has told the harbour master of my estimated time of arrival and my need to make repairs.

On my approach I could see the ship, *Holmdale*, up against the jetty. I got through to the mate, a Welshman from Montgomery, who told me to go behind him, and round to the quay. They took my ropes and made me fast. About thirty of the locals were loading the ship with wool and frozen fish. They watched me come ashore and I met the female harbour master, Robyn Pohio, who suggested that I should go round to the fisherman's wharf, where the boat would be safer. A couple of lads leapt on board, I motored round and they made me fast. She invited me to her house for tea and a shower, which I badly needed. I went back with her and met her husband Mike, a cray-fisherman. They invited me to stay for dinner and said I would be welcome to their spare room. The prospect of a non-moving bed

133

was terrific and I stayed with them for ten days. Mike helped me tremendously with all the jobs on the boat. I mended the sail by hand in their sitting room, we repaired the forestay and put a gate valve on the bilge pump so that water will no longer leak back when it's rough. One night we were having a drink on board when we heard running water. The loo was flooding over. We stopped it by turning off the seacock, and took it to pieces to find a broken spring on one of the valves. I wasn't able to repair it properly, but put in a new valve.

Every day people would ring and invite me round. I went to the ham radio operator's house for dinner with the postmaster and his wife, and one night to the Johansens', descendants of a ship's captain who was wrecked over a hundred years ago. They have an estate on the middle of the island, farming about 4,000 acres, and breed racehorses and sheep. I had a pleasant evening. Visitors are so few and far between that one's every word is listened to with interest.

I met Lee Clough and his wife Diana. I'd arrived penniless and there is no bank on the island but Diana offered to cash a cheque for me, as she was about to visit England. Lee kindly offered to clean the bottom of the boat which was covered with barnacles. He is a professional diver for the most expensive shellfish in the world, abalone. He showed me the seal colony and some Moriori tree carvings which are in the north of the island. The Morioris were the original settlers, peaceful people. When invaded they were so passive that they let the Maoris kill and eat them. I saw a statue of the last true Moriori, Tommy Solomon – a big man, weighing 32 stone. When he died they had to remove a window frame to get him out of the house.

The islanders gave me stacks of frozen meat and fish and the fridge was full. When I was ready to leave the policeman came to clear my boat for customs. It was a wonderful send-off. There were so many presents. Mike's neighbour gave me a cake, and Helen, a Maori girl, gave me two salamis, carrots and spinach. These are scarce on the island and very expensive, as so much has to be sent in from the mainland. It was all much appreciated.

I left in a nice little breeze, motored round to the south of the island and then motor-sailed for a couple of hours before nightfall, through the channel between Pit Island and Chatham. I switched off the engine and after a couple of drinks went to bed, waking several times during the night to check the course. She was sailing nicely. The current must have lifted me slightly north because I went within ten miles of a cluster of rocks. I slipped past them, without knowing it, while asleep. In the morning I was sick and had a headache. I'd eaten some of Helen's salami. Perhaps it was that.

DAY TWO: 2 DECEMBER 1987

I still feel sick but am getting over the headache. I feel tired all the time, in spite of having slept and slept. When I woke this morning she was sailing nicely on a broad reach, the wind was coming from the north and gradually went round to the north-west. I eased the sheets, and went along beautifully, full and bye. A nice day but a big cluster of cloud on the horizon. I watched as it came closer and thought that it was going to miss me but the wind started to pick up. I put on my heavy weather gear and safety harness and went out into the rain. Before I could reef in the sails I found myself in the middle of a violent squall lasting for only fifteen minutes. During that time the boat was racing along while I was trying to reef. I got the staysail in, started to furl the jib but the wind was too strong. I couldn't get the reefing line pulled in, but put it on a winch and started winding it in slowly with the sail flogging away. I felt the line go light and by the noise I knew what had happened: the sail had flown to pieces. The clew pulled right out of the panels and ripped the edging of the sail to about halfway up. It was a hell of a mess, bits of sail flapping about everywhere. Easing the main sheet, I set the self-steering to run downwind and in another five minutes it was all over. I was absolutely sickened by it. Losing one of my working sails on the second day will take the edge off my sailing. Feeling pretty desperate I tried to take down the sail and failed. I was unable to unravel it before pulling it off the furling gear. I tried and couldn't do it. So I rested for a while.

A few hours later I managed to unwind it and get it off. I have at least got a spare staysail, and although it's much smaller I put it up. It wouldn't furl because the halyard was wrapping itself around the stay; the head of the sail was too far down with about ten feet left at the top. I tried it further up, but it didn't work; it was a little triangle at the top of the mast. I decided to take it down and put it away in the locker with the ripped sail.

I racked my brains on how to fit the sail, and eventually it came to me. I must put a line from the head of the sail up to the swivel, making

135

up for the shortness of it. The first time I tried, the line was too long. I pulled the sail down again, shortened the line, and it worked. All I have to do when I use it is to move the sheet further back, finding a position where the sail will set best. Once again I have two headsails, but as one is so small I shall lose power. I'll have to do my best with what I've got.

I'm running downwind, goosewinged at about 2.5 knots. Perfect spinnaker weather, but I'm feeling exhausted. It's a funny old day, overcast with a bit of rain every now and again and a light wind from the west. It needs to be stronger to hold everything taut. The sails are slatting around.

DAY THREE: MY POSITION 44° 28′S 170° 58′W

Going along quite nicely at about four knots, heading slightly south of east. Every now and again the wind gets a bit light and there are pockets of fog. When I woke up this morning visibility was only 200 yards. It's now about half a mile, but I'm getting a little brightness from the sun, putting in about 1.5 amps into the batteries.

I had to sling out a lot of the food that was given me. After I was sick, I threw the salamis over the side. The crayfish had thawed out and joined them and some of the meat went too. I couldn't eat all that food in the first few days. I tried to tell them, but they were so generous and wouldn't listen. I've kept some steak and fish in the fridge but have more faith in tins. If I got food poisoning out here, it could be fairly final!

I switched off the engine when leaving the Chatham Islands and clouds of smoke came out of the engine room. The belts must have been slipping although they looked in reasonable shape. I shall have to adjust them but won't think about it yet. I just want to get in some sailing. The batteries seem to be staying up pretty well; I might use the Mase tomorrow but as there's some sunshine they'll pick up again. To save power I sleep with only a hurricane lamp in the pilot house. Not that anyone would see me in this fog.

I'm still a little apprehensive about the Horn. So far, at this latitude the winds have been quite light. I'm coming up to 45°S and have only to do another 11°S to get around. I hope to get a decent run and some reasonable weather. It would make a nice change.

DAY FOUR: 4 DECEMBER 1987

It's Friday, gale force eight and my position is 44° 55′S 168° 28′W. That's quite a leap overnight. The wind's coming from the north-west and I've been nipping along at 6.5 knots, sometimes 7, reefed right down. She tries to come up to the wind occasionally, which is awkward. I shall try to steer true east if I can.

I've been sick again and am feeling generally rough. Everything takes a lot of effort. I had to throw out a lot more meat and fish, it had thawed out and was bleeding everywhere. Quite a mess. I was going to cook some of it today but it's too rough, so instead I got out a tin of Irish stew and had that.

Started reading Joshua Slocum's book again, *Sailing Alone Around The World*. I first read it when I was building the hull, and thought I should know more about him and his circumnavigation. It is delightfully written; he is such a happy character, and what a sailor! It makes me look pale. He'd be disgusted with my performance. I hung on to as much sail as I could today, but others would be sailing full out. Joshua Slocum uses lovely expressions: 'a capful of wind'. I like that. He wasn't frightened with a capful of wind.

I've been up since about four when it was almost daylight. The nights are getting shorter. I'm going along at 3 knots in light winds. There's a nasty swell left over from yesterday's blow but the glass has dropped still more, down to 985 millibars, the lowest for a long time. I've been waiting since last night for something to happen. Before going to bed I took the main down and used only the two headsails, as I felt sure it was going to blow up from the south. I thought I was in the middle of a low, but if so it is slow-moving because as yet nothing has happened. The wind has gone round a little more to the west and I'm now on a single headsail with the wind on the port quarter. I'd be very pleased to see the glass rise again.

In retrospect I think I could have sailed all night on the main, but I was frightened of losing another sail, which I can't afford. If I had a crew member I'd be on the spinnaker for a couple of hours, but I can't face doing it alone, which is frustrating. The incident with the sail the other day should never have happened. I didn't have the strength to get it in. I must repair it in the Falklands, it's too big a job to tackle on the boat. I might be able to recut the old jib into a staysail and give myself enough sail to get home.

I'm still waiting for the onslaught. I put the main up an hour ago and the seas are quite nasty. Thinking I wasn't going fast enough I took one reef out. A squall came up, and not wanting to be caught out I put it back in again. I then had to take down the main completely. If the wind changes violently I'm better off with the headsails.

DAY FIVE

I made 115 miles yesterday and the other half of the gale is here at last. I was beginning to wonder whether I should put up more sail when suddenly the barometer went up, and the wind and big seas are following, luckily on one quarter. She's holding a fairly good course on a small amount of staysail but even that worries me after losing one. I could go faster if I put out more sail but dare not chance it. It won't make much difference, perhaps a few more days overall, and I'll be quicker if I manage to hold everything together.

DAY SIX

Still bombing along in the gale. Wind on the quarter, glass dropped again; I don't know what's going on. Perhaps two lows in quick succession because the wind's gone back to the north-north-west. It was coming from the south-west last night. I simply don't know. Because of the storm I'm finding it difficult to eat. I had a cup of coffee this morning and will try to get around to food later. I sometimes wonder what I'm doing out here but at least I'm making progress in the right direction. I'm happy to hold this latitude until I'm about halfway across and will then go down gradually. It will be a few hundred miles further, but I'm thinking of my comfort. It would be so much colder in the ice belt.

Since leaving Chatham I've not used navigation lights and haven't kept a lookout. I've given up because half the time I can't see anything. The waves are so big, and for two days there was too much fog to see anyway. I don't think there are too many ships around here. At least I hope not. It may be bad seamanship but I'm trying to save energy for later in the voyage, when I think I will need it. I'll put on the lights when nearer Cape Horn because that's where traffic would start converging. I suspect that most big ships go through the Magellan Straits, unless going direct to Cape Town.

There's a peculiar phenomenon on board. When the boat rolls there is terrific interference on the radio, a very fierce crackling. I was listening to a programme when a wave hit the side of the boat. Foam flew all over the deck and the crackling continued until it had cleared. The French have recently exploded an atomic bomb up north and I wonder if the fall-out could be carried this way by the current. I've been using sea water to cook my potatoes but will now stick to fresh and not take any chances.

DAY SEVEN

Midday and I've been at sea a week. It's still blasting away out there. I'm down to 45° 17'S 161° 57'W, and I'm exhausted because I'm being thrown around all the time. We have been knocked down once again and I got pretty uptight, frightened. The power of the sea when it's like this is incredible. With the wind howling outside and the waves hitting the side of the boat, if someone were out there striking the steel hull with a sledge-hammer I wouldn't be able to hear him. My mind is numb with solitude. I find it difficult to think.

I had to go outside earlier to correct the steering and did some filming, poked my head out and swung the camera in several directions. I hope it will give Bob something to go on with. Ideally I should leave it out for about an hour, but it wouldn't do the camera much good. I desperately need a few days of quiet sailing as I don't know how much longer I can keep it up. I just know I've got to, I'm out on a limb. I could go north into quieter waters and if I get too tired I'll consider it. I'm hoping against hope things will quieten down.

The barometer has gone up 2 millibars. Not very much. This is the third day of the gale and I'm making good progress in the right direction but not as much as I could with less wind. I did 80 miles yesterday and the day before that about 95. My average for the week is 682, so I'm not far below what I'd planned. This should be quite a run because I've been screaming along most of the day. It's still blowing like hell out there.

I had a chat last night with a radio amateur in Australia, Jack, who left Wales when he was twelve. We talked about Cardigan where he'd spent his childhood. It was very nice indeed. We'll keep in touch if we can.

The sea is rough and frightening. About half an hour ago there was

139

white foam as far as I could see, as white as snow, so bright that I needed dark glasses, so fierce that it whipped off the top of the waves. The glass has gone up again so it must be passing through slowly. I got wet a short while ago. Two of the boards were in, the louvre doors shut, and I was sitting on the bench seat. A wave whipped over, filled up the cockpit and slopped through into my lap. I went out to correct the steering, and the sea hit and soaked me. More clothes to dry. I dry them out a bit and then wear them and steam off. Once they're wet with salt there's nothing you can do – they'll always feel damp.

I hope the wind doesn't die away completely when this storm is over. The seas are coming from two directions now, one from the south and the other from the south-west. Yesterday it came from the north as well: big combers.

What a storm! It's morning now. The wind howled last night and got up to force eleven. The seas are horrific and the glass has gone up by 25 millibars in the last twenty-four hours. It is still rising. It's desperately cold and the wind's coming up from the south. It was time for prayers last night. I haven't prayed so hard in my life.

10

Now for Cape Horn

DAY NINE: 9 DECEMBER 1987

After that storm I think *Zane Spray* can handle anything; however, I'm not so sure about me. She stood up to the worst that I've seen and survived without damage. I have been moving in the right direction throughout the gales but could get a bit of speed up, given a spot of nice weather. It looks as though it might be settling now and I hope to get the main up later today.

My position is 44° 37'S 157° 46'W, and making good progress. The barometer went up to 1022 which is quite a rise from the low point during the storm. There's a strong wind blowing from the north-west because of all this high pressure. I'm going along at 6 knots with three reefs in the main and a bit of the small jib out. I've done 138 miles in the last twenty-four hours, so the speed has picked up beautifully.

DAY TEN

Going along nicely, on course. Not a bad run, keeping up a good average. It's a bright sunny day and she's dancing along, covering a lot of ground. The position at lunchtime was 45° 33'S 154° 31'W, so it's under 90° now to get to Cape Horn.

I took the last steak out of the fridge which I'll have tonight. The log reads, 'Out of Scotch, gin and rum. Some beer left, wine for

141

Christmas and a bottle of champagne for the Horn.'

I managed to make contact with Jean Price in Anglesey. I was unable to speak to her but relayed a couple of messages via New Zealand. As she knows Eric, I should get a reasonable amount of information back home.

SUNDAY 13 DECEMBER 1987

I'm bombing along, goosewinged with a westerly wind. It's a beautiful day, an icy light wind coming from the west and right up my tail. I'm heading due east. I let the average slip last night as I'd had a pretty hard time with gusty winds from the south, and had to take the main down in the small hours. I was frozen and very tired. Yesterday I sailed slowly. I could have put more sail up but left it until this morning. I've done 1,420 miles in thirteen days, not bad at all. But I shan't make the Horn by Christmas. Sometime though. Here's hoping I get there.

Sorted out some warm clothes which I'll need later on. I'm still wearing what I left in – apart from my underpants, ceremoniously buried at sea. I had a couple of bacon and egg sandwiches with bread I made a couple of days ago. It was very nice.

I'm in better spirits than at the end of the first week. This is quite usual and whatever the sickness was has passed. I feel pretty good. Tired, but maybe that's the fresh air. There is one can of beer left which I'll polish off tonight. Plenty of soft drinks. John, the milkman in Mooloolaba, got me fruit juice, orange and apple, which should last me a long time. I've still got some blue cod, but whether or not I shall get around to using it, I don't know. I'll have to have a good sniff to make sure it's still eatable.

DAY SIXTEEN: 16 DECEMBER 1987 IN THE AFTERNOON

It was lovely early this morning but the wind went light and started to go round to the north-east and then there was drizzle. It's now very overcast and the wind is trying to get round further to the east. My compass course is south-east but, with the magnetic variation of 27° on top of that, I'm heading almost south. I'm doing only about 3 knots, and tried on the other tack but it wasn't a good course, so I might as well go south and see what happens later on. It's not too cold and pretty calm, a big swell but no breakers, quite a reasonable sea.

I'm halfway across the Southern Ocean in sixteen days which seems incredible. As I go south, because the lines of longitude are closer, the distance decreases. I might be able to do it in a reasonable time, depending on weather conditions. I'm down to 47° 50′S 138° 29′W and beginning to get near the ice, the northernmost limit it gets to. I could meet icebergs anywhere now. I shall cut through an area of ice, and hope for good visibility, with moonlit nights. I'll have to keep a pretty good lookout.

It seems to be going fairly well. Today is the first time that I've had the wind forward of the beam since leaving Chatham Island and apart from the storm, which terrified me, and a couple of average gales, it has been a good run. My prayers have been answered. I've certainly had good weather.

DAY SEVENTEEN

Freezing cold. The night was bitter, wet and nasty. This isn't a place to hang around in. Scott has my total admiration. I can well understand Oates wandering off into the night. What a dismal place, and I'm further north than they were. I'm feeling a bit out on a limb. Two thousand miles from land, unless one counts Antarctica.

19 DECEMBER

While I was waiting to contact Jean this morning, Paul came on the air loud and clear. He had flown to Brazil to get married, was in a hotel in Rio with a portable radio, transmitting on a wire antenna hanging out of the window. It was early on his wedding day, he was late, but I was able to wish him well from the Roaring Forties.

DAY TWENTY: 20 DECEMBER 1987

The position at midday was 48° 09′S 131° 18′W. Making good progress in large seas with a strong wind from slightly south of west. I'm on three-quarters of the staysail, doing 5 knots on quite a good course. This section has taken longer than I expected after a strong blow from the north-east. I was hard on the wind trying to go east when it went

143

round in a circle and headed me. I took the main down early yesterday which slowed me down a bit. The wind was so unpredictable that it was easier just to run on headsails and go downwind as much as possible. The wind's stronger today, the barometer's still high and I believe there's going to be another low following.

I've a bit of a headache and felt sick, so took some anti-seasickness pills. It's a job to keep warm and my feet seem to be cold most of the time. I can't find any gloves, but if it gets bad I'll make some by cutting holes in a pair of socks. I've been on deck in the cold adjusting the sails, but can't go out without getting wet which means getting into heavy weather gear each time.

I'm still reading Joshua Slocum's book. It's a lovely tale and there's so much that I can relate to now. Not that I think that I'm anything like him, he was a real sailor. It's the places we've been to and the sort of things that happen.

I've started a paperback given to me by Derek the plumber from home. He gave me several books, one of them *The Eye of the Fleet*; I'm quite enjoying it. Maybe I'll get stuck into reading now. It would be the first time in my life. There's not much else to do.

DAY TWENTY-TWO: 22 DECEMBER 1987

It's Tuesday and the wind is heading me from the east and keeps dodging around. I'm having a job to scrape a good course. I'm heading south-eastish, more south than east. My position at noon was 48° 22′S 126° 52′W and I've covered a total of 2,144 miles in twenty-one days. Just above 100 miles a day, but I could do with a bit more as my average has been falling in the last week.

I picked up a weather forecast and there's a bit of a high pressure system somewhere behind me. I think the centre is at 40°S and is travelling this way slowly. I hope there are westerlies at the bottom of it but will have to wait and see. I'm halfway across now, and need a bit of south but had hoped to do it more gradually. I could make it in another twenty days. I'm getting lazy, reading a lot and not doing much around the boat which is damp and cold. I'm only warm in my sleeping bag or when I heat the kettle and stick my feet on it, that warms me up a bit. Having the fridge on just takes the chill off the air in the cabin. It sounds mad, but without the warm air from the back of the fridge it would be unbearable. Not the place to be, this part of he world. I'll be happy when I start heading north again.

24 DECEMBER 1987

n New Zealand, Australia and on the other side of the date line it is
hristmas Day. Madeleine will be asleep in South Africa – it's today
ere still I suppose; it's most confusing. I had a good morning's run
nd not a bad night's sailing either. I had to reef down last night
ecause she started getting lively, up to 8 knots and I'm well into the
eberg area now. I was worried at the thought of hitting one at that
peed, so slowed down to about 5. I don't suppose that would have
ade much difference, but I went to sleep.

I woke this morning to a beautiful clear sky. The wind had gone
ound and I was heading north. I think I'd not been going that way
ong and straightened her up. The wind got stronger until I was doing
knots again. I reefed down a bit and that's how we've been ever
nce, going along splendidly. The day's run up picked up to 110 miles.

CHRISTMAS EVE

ve still got the bottle of wine. I might have it this evening, will make
p my mind later on. I hope this progress keeps up for a couple of
ays; if the wind stays steady it will be beautiful. I have to reef down
hen it's gusty and a lot of the time I'm not going fast enough because
can't do it quickly; it takes me longer to do it than if I was fit. I'm a
it late for Cape Horn at Christmas. I lost two and a half weeks going
a to the Chathams but would probably still have been late. Never
ind, it's not a race. I'll just get there and look forward to a rest and
nice warm shower when I reach the Falklands. I hope they can
ccommodate me; it would have to be in a private house as there isn't
yacht club.

I haven't done the Christmas decorations yet; perhaps I'll do it this
vening. I feel a bit sad at the thought of putting them up on my own.
his will be the first Christmas I've spent alone. I've had more than
ne in hospital but always with other people. Never mind.

CHRISTMAS DAY

Had a good QSO with Cape Town last night. It was their Christmas morning and my Christmas Eve. I gave my position, which will be passed on to Madeleine via Jennie. And I got through to Peter Shor in the Falklands.

There's a howler going on out there. Strong winds from the north all day yesterday and some good sailing. Last night for a while there was a bit of moon, which would be handy for the Horn. I reefed down and slept fitfully. Not a good night, quite rough with squalls. This morning I reefed down the headsails a bit more, have been careering along and chalked up 130 miles in the last twenty-four hours. My position today is 49° 27'S 119° 01'W. It's fine as long as I'm going fast to the east, as I can soon make a bit of south, at least I think I can. need about 2° at this point, but as I'm amongst icebergs it may be sensible to carry on at this latitude for a few days. I'll see how it goes. I have not yet seen any ice and doubt that I would in seas this high, certainly not at night.

I don't think there will be much festivity today. I took out the decorations that we had last year but have put up only the Christmas Tree and a Father Christmas cut-out made by Jennie. I'm 2,000 miles from anywhere, cold and bleak, but making good progress. I was going to make a feast with a tin of chunky chicken, but can't make up my mind.

DAY THIRTY: 30 DECEMBER 1987

My position is 51° 02'S 102° 59'W. It's been grey, cold and wet since Christmas with strong winds at near gale force. I've been tacking downwind, going well, east all the time, goosewinged with two small headsails, and running. With a bit of luck I could be at the Horn in about fourteen days. I hope the weather is decent when I go around. I've had a rough old time over the last few days, so cold at nights it's difficult to keep warm. I won't be sorry to get back to a more civilized latitude in the Atlantic. Oh, for a bit of sun on my back! I've found myself at a loose end and a bit bored on this stretch, as it's been too rough to do any work on the boat. I've read all the books, so it's just a case of keeping myself fit, playing patience, sleeping and finding out where I am. That's about all I can do. I get the BBC World Service quite well, and probably pick up what they get in the Falklands and North America because it goes out at peculiar times. I'm upside-down in time. It's 18.00 hours GMT now, but seven o'clock in the morning for me. Everyone else has had their New Year's Eve but mine doesn't come until midnight tonight.

31 DECEMBER 1987

Log reads, 'Happy New Year, Dai. Ta. Cold. Full gale blowing.'

I hit a piece of ice at 5 knots in the night, a submerged iceberg. I believe they are known as growlers. I was asleep in the fore-cabin trying to keep warm, and there was a hell of a bang. I sat up in the darkness, half-asleep, and found the hull shaking and creaking. I crawled along the side of the cabin, trying to work out where everything was. She had listed over to the weather-side and stayed there, and by the time I'd got to the cockpit was coming back upright, groaning as she did so. I couldn't see anything in the darkness and won't know whether the boat is dented until I next take her out of the water.

For the last week I've been in the large area of ice going north into the Pacific. In about 180 miles I'll be out of it until I reach Cape Horn. I'll be glad, because the thought of running into a really big iceberg at night is horrifying. I wouldn't be able to see one even if I kept a lookout, as there is no moonlight, just cloud.

I've been struggling unsuccessfully to get her to sail downwind this morning, I don't know what's wrong. Maybe there's too much play in the self-steering. I don't know. I'm well reefed down with the minutest amount of sail up, doing between 3 and 4 knots, generally in the right direction, but she keeps going off course and backs the sails. The seas are pretty big and still from two directions, and that could be throwing her about. I've been out in the cold for about three hours and must have a break and let her get on with it. It doesn't really matter much where I'm steering as there's still about 1,100 miles before the Horn.

147

DAY THIRTY-FOUR: 3 JANUARY 1988

My position is 52° 39'S 95° 22'W. Making good progress. It's Sunday I think, and a beautiful day. When I woke this morning I was nearly becalmed. It was very pleasant: the motion was nice and gentle with just enough wind to keep the sails full. I shook out the reefs and got her going and she's been sailing very smoothly all morning at about 4 knots. I filmed myself sticking a patch on the staysail, then cleaned the gas cooker, aired the bedding, topped up and charged the batteries, swept the floor and had a couple of boiled eggs with toast. The sun makes one hell of a difference to the way I feel. Progress is fantastic, more than three-quarters of the way in thirty-four days.

Last night's run was very good and yesterday's not bad either. started out on full sail, it gradually got cloudy and the wind started to strengthen so I put in first one reef, then two and finally three.

4 JANUARY 1988

Last night as I went to bed I wondered if I should take the main down and go only on the headsails, but decided to leave it and see how she went. She managed between 5 and 6 knots all night which is what I'm doing now. When I woke the wind had gone round to the north west and I was heading north. I put her back on course, running downwind, with a full main and headsails.

Dolphins are playing with the boat: the first I've seen since the tropics. On this crossing my only companions have been birds.

DAY THIRTY-SIX

This morning it's foggy but above it the sky is fairly clear. I can see the sun which is nice, but I'm back to sailing in a goldfish bowl. Reed's *Nautical Almanac* gives several possible alternatives for foggy conditions: standing on deck sounding the foghorn, banging a sauce pan with a spoon, or as a last resort starting a tar fire on deck. I'm trying to imagine myself standing here in thick fog beating a saucepan a thousand miles from anywhere. A nice thought.

My position is 53° 17'S 90° 19'W which is pretty good. The difference between my time and GMT is only six hours now and closing. think it will be four hours ahead by the time I reach the Falklands

rst flying fish.

w: An albatross paddling past and overtaking
ecalmed *Zane Spray*.

m: This broken boom gave me quite a
ache.

Jennie inspecting my labours on the mast. Thirsty work.

Jennie squatting on a pontoon, painting the hull.

...tmas Day 1986. All decorations, including the hat, made by Jennie from wine bags and ...oard.

...y welcome tow into Wollongong, courtesy of the police.

The HTV crew filming on board
Lavender Bay, Sydney.

Zane Spray in Sydney Harbour,
1987.

fway circumnavigator.

ainted *Zane Spray*. Birkenhead, Sydney.

Testing the new spinnaker on the
to Lord Howe Island.

Approaching Cape Horn with seas
as flat as they seem. I had to take
photographs from the top of a wav
order to see the Horn (just visible
the horizon).

...s painting of my voyage on the Marina wall in Horta, the Azores.

...ng into harbour at Aberaeron after three years voyaging.

Recognizing friends [in] crowd of thousands.

Llangeitho's welcome. Home at last.

I'm about 800 miles from Cape Horn and beginning to notch it down. I hope it will be fine enough to film when I go round. It would be terrible if I didn't actually see anything.

DAY THIRTY-SEVEN

I did 108 miles last night and in thirty-seven days have covered 3,845 miles. I tried to start the engine for the first time since leaving the Chathams and found a burnt-out wire on the starter solenoid. I replaced it with a thicker one and she started immediately, purring away for an hour, which charged the batteries. It's just as well to make sure everything's working. I've had every sort of condition in the last few days: light winds, almost becalmed, fog, strong winds, but it's been good stuff apart from the really nasty blow earlier on.

I'm only 360 miles from Cape Pila, at the western entrance to the Magellan Straits. I'm not going that way but heading straight south. I'm the nearest I've been to land for a long, long time, making good progress and a good course with strong winds from the north-west. By the time I get to 70°W I want to be at 56° 15′S, which would put me just in line to clear land going round the Horn.

I seem to be weathering it all quite well and am eating sensibly. Had the last of the blue cod in batter with dried peas and boiled potatoes – very nice – followed by pancakes made from the left-over batter. The gas ran out and I had to change the bottle. I've still got one left, but might need to get a refill in the Falklands for my return home.

DAY FORTY-ONE

My position is 55° 14′S 77° 06′W. It's funny how a limerick can drive you nearly mad. One is going around my head like looped supermarket music:

> There was an old man of Cape Horn,
>
> Who wished that he hadn't been born,
>
> He wouldn't have bin,

149

But the rubber was thin,

And in one place was actually torn.

DAY FORTY-TWO

I'm south of Chile, the coast is about sixty miles to the north. I've been becalmed for the last four hours in bright sunshine on a sea of glass: unbelievable. The boat is tidy, everything loose has been stowed away and tied down for what life may bring in the next few days. I made some bread and had a good meal: the condemned man. As I went on deck to throw a tin overboard, a whale with a calf surfaced about fifty feet behind the boat. I grabbed the camera and managed to film them. Dolphins were playing with the whale: it was such a peaceful scene that I found it hard to think of what Cape Horn might hold.

The barometer started to drop quickly, the wind came from the north: the start of yet another gale. On the still, flat seas, *Zane Spray* under full sail is making a fast approach to the Horn. Timing seems to be perfect for a sight of land at first light tomorrow. I rested, knowing I would need all my strength during the next days.

DAY FORTY-THREE

On the horizon I can see three enormous peaks to the north. They must be right back in the Andes. They aren't clouds, as they are the wrong shape. I'm going along quite nicely and the wind's coming from the north-west at force six. My position is 56° 04′S 70° 20′W and I'm heading between the islands of Ildefonso and Diego Ramirez, two groups about sixty miles to the west of the Horn. I'm going fairly close to the northern one as I'm no longer on a lee shore. That will put me on a good course. Tomorrow, with any luck. Tomorrow. Creaming around with a glass of champagne in my hand. Force four from the west would do nicely. We shall see.

DAY FORTY-FOUR: 14 JANUARY 1988

The glass is still dropping, the gale has started, but I'm here. I've been lucky. A good approach before the seas had time to get too bad. It's certainly rough now and pretty grim in the rain. I'm trying to sail closer to Cape Horn, which might take me into a bit of sheltered water. Or it might not. I'm still eight miles to the south.

MIDDAY

I'm a Cape Horner. I'm going to be a pain in the arse when I get back to the yacht club, leaning on the bar, holding forth to all who will listen. I opened the carefully saved bottle of champagne, toasted the Horn and thought of my great-grandfather, skipper of a square-rigger, a Cape Horner many times. I used to read his charts as a small boy in the apple loft at Rosemount in Llanon. Over the side went the glass, and the bottle with a message inside. My salute to Cape Horn.

11

Sun on My Back

I tried to sail up closer to the Horn, but the weather closed in with icy rain and squalls. Losing sight of land, I made a course to the east to get off the shallow continental shelf and back in deep water.

DAY FORTY-SEVEN

After a good run for the first twenty-four hours, by evening I was up by Isla de los Estados in a full-blown gale which carried on through the night. Without the main and using only two bits of headsail I was still doing 6 knots, but by morning had come down to 3. I waited until it was warmer, put the main up, and am now under full sail. The barometer's risen 11 millibars. I'd begun to think the needle had dropped off.

I'm now halfway to the Falklands from the Horn: I might do it in another couple of days. It's been a lovely morning but is becoming a little overcast, the seas are still big and not breaking – little white horses here and there.

I ran the engine for an hour but she started with difficulty, probably owing to the cold. The wind generator is not working and is one of the things I must sort out in the Falklands. There's a long list of work to be done. I must get the boat ready for the next leg, which is about as long as the one I'm on. From St Helena to the Azores is about as long again. I've got to do more than twice the distance I've achieved so far, before being within striking distance of home. Most of it will be in the tropics and it will be lovely to have some sun on my back again.

I'm looking forward to Stanley and having a good hot bath with a bottle of Scotch in my hand. Yes, that would go down well. I like the idea very much. It was quite tough rounding the Horn and a tough forty-eight hours afterwards – in fact, until this morning. The joy of doing it hasn't yet sunk in, but it's beginning to. And I'm very happy to be back in the Atlantic even though it is so cold. I'm heading north again and every degree north is good.

At midday I was 53° 57'S 61° 24'W. Land Ho! Land Ho! Bechain Island is in sight, thirty miles south of the Falklands. I'm motoring to recharge the batteries, get past the island and on to a reasonably safe course before nightfall. There's very little wind at the moment. I thought I would motor as I was doing only 1.5 knots. It's been a lovely warm day, and the first time for ages that I've been out in the air without my clothes on. I thoroughly aired everything, did some washing, swept the carpets and tidied the boat in readiness for going ashore.

DAY FORTY-NINE

The wind came up this morning and I was pinching a course to try to keep off the Falklands. It gradually came round to the south-east and I had about an hour's sleep. Luckily I woke to find her bombing along; I need to keep up 5 knots to get in before dark. I had been wondering whether to motor today or wait until tomorrow before going in. It looks as though the decision has been made for me.

I was on the radio this morning to Al Wilson in New Zealand and to Jean in Wales who will tell Gillian that I'm around the Horn and almost at Stanley. I can see Sea Lion Island in the distance but not, as yet, the mainland. I've seen nothing of the Navy and can't get in touch on the VHF. Is it possible for a 36-foot steel boat to creep in under the radar, or am I being watched?

I sailed in between two rocky isles and the lighthouse, turned into the Sound and motor-sailed the two miles between the rocky shores, looking for the entrance to the harbour. The icy wind was heading me at force seven and I stowed the sails ready to enter Port Stanley, freezing cold and very wet as the sea was choppy and spray was coming over the top. Suddenly the engine's revs changed. I couldn't believe it was happening as, once again, the engine cut out. I tried to restart her but she wouldn't fire. Drifting backwards in the strong wind towards a rocky lee shore, I put out the jib, and very slowly, sailed towards the sea again: my safest course.

I put out a PAN (an emergency without danger to life) call, in the hope of raising some help, and was answered straight away. The fisheries' protection boat, the *Worra*, would come and tow me in. Managing to sail into a cove, Hell's Kitchen, I dropped anchor to wait for them. The anchor dragged and wouldn't take until I was a hundred yards from the white sandy shore. I sat on deck looking at the lovely sands. I decided that if the anchor dragged I would go ashore and walk on the beach. Fortunately I didn't. It happened to be a minefield. I was told later that a great deal of the island is still mined. The Argentinian helicopters had dropped plastic devices which are virtually undetectable and there is no record of where they are. They get washed around on the beach. I was lucky.

When the *Worra* arrived, one of the crew came on board and took the wheel while I made him tea and stayed in the warm cabin. They put me up against the jetty and helped me make the ropes fast before I was welcomed by the harbour master, Les Halliday, who said that they had been waiting for me and were very concerned as I was so long overdue. They were beginning to wonder what had happened. The messages saying that I had gone into the Chatham Islands for repairs had not filtered through. Les and a policewoman came aboard and we went through the paperwork which was nice and easy. He invited me home for a hot bath and a meal and I bought a bottle of Scotch on the way. I could have murdered one.

Les's wife, Peggy, very kindly did all my washing and lent me her sewing machine to repair the sails. Mine was still not working. I met Graham Oakes from South Wales, working in the pathology department of the local hospital, who let me mend them at his house. He had not properly moved in, so there was plenty of space. The crews of both a Danish and a Canadian yacht worked alongside me as they had repairs to do. I glued the jib together with canvas on each side and sewed it, which made it so heavy and stiff that it would take a gale to fill it.

One radio news report about my arrival had already gone out and another interview on the voyage was broadcast the following night.

154

This was subsequently heard by General Carlier, who took part in the first Whitbread Race, and he sent a message saying that he'd like to meet me. Les, who also is the customs officer at the airport, took me to Army Headquarters at Mount Pleasant. We had lunch in the Officers' Mess and then went to see the general, an extremely pleasant man. I asked him if he knew Peter Blake, who had been in all the Whitbread Races. I told him about my telling Peter that I'd been involved in two of the Whitbread Round-the-World races. I had left home three weeks before the second race started and by the time I reached Cape Town they were all home. That's now happened twice. It was a very relaxed meeting and we talked about sailing. As we walked out of his room into the office he said, 'You know, David, I'd love to swap places with you. Would you care to take on my job?' I replied, 'Not really sir, I'd have to cut my hair.' My shoulder-length locks got a funny look from the sergeant.

I had a letter from Joy Cook in Sydney, saying that she has developed cancer. It is hard to understand that someone who has given her life to nursing and looking after others should be so ill. She asked me to tell her how I had managed to survive and to give her help. I thought about it for several days, not wanting to say the wrong thing, and then told her to take each day as it comes: today is the best you've got and tomorrow may be better.

It was a nice interlude, wining and dining on each other's boats. My only problem was the cold: it was freezing there. At night my feet were like ice and I had to sleep in my clothes. I was able to put the fridge on again as the Army had promised me some gas. They were extremely generous and a great help, trying to fix the generator and wind charger and supplying me with food and drinks for practically nothing for the next leg of the journey. The officer who took me to the warehouse, John Edgar, asked the catering officer if he had any sea-dump cans. The catering officer looked extremely puzzled and John said, 'Well then, what about dented tins?' The penny dropped and he realized that something was wanted for nothing.

There were gales for the three days before I left. The Danish boat was on the outside of *Zane Spray* and we both took quite a hammering. My boat was leaping out of the water so far that the keel could be seen underneath her, to where the mast is stepped. She was right up against the jetty and got quite a big dent in the port side, and her safety rails were broken. Kim, the skipper of the Danish yacht, with Bob Macleod,

155

a radio ham who lives in the town, looked after my boat while I was out during the worst of the gales. I had gone to tea at the Rectory with the vicar and then to the church service. When I got back the worst was over. They were glad that I hadn't been there, as I would have been worried sick. Out of the cold, in the cabin, we polished off a bottle of Scotch. As we finished it the wind went down. I slept well into the next day.

I sailed on a beautiful day. Les and Peggy came to see me off with my departure papers and a list of positions and sightings of icebergs, stretching some 700 miles to the north of the Falklands. One iceberg, measuring three miles by two, was reported to be on the course that I was taking. The *Worra*, who had towed me in, came to escort me out. Hans Steinicke and Lydia Wollersheim on the Canadian yacht, *Irene*, had rounded Cape Horn a few hours before me and left on the same day. They sailed up from another jetty and waited for Kim, who was tied up to me, to cast off. When he had done so, my engine wouldn't start. It was too cold. I hadn't tried to start it before for fear of covering Kim's boat in soot. It had been fine a few days earlier. I sailed off the quay and timed it just right, casting off the last warp as the bow was swinging from the quay, and nipping back to the wheel. As the main was already up she drifted away. I brought her about and Sean from the *Worra* asked if he could come aboard. He jumped on and helped me to put out the rest of the sails. I showed him how the self-steering worked and we coasted down Stanley Harbour and past Kitty Burton's house, giving a blast on the horn. Kitty is the widow of an ex-whaler and had given me a rope puzzle, made by her husband, to keep me busy at sea. Sean stayed on board while we sailed away from the harbour and into the Sound, then the *Worra* took him off and the wind died before I was out in the open sea. I tried to start the engine again, this time she fired, and I motored for an hour.

I started sailing again with a good stiff breeze from the north-west. She was going along great guns and the *Irene* was only three-quarters of a mile ahead of me. The wind was a bit strong for the self-steering and so I put a reef in the main. As dusk came I reefed in a headsail to slow her down and make her more comfortable for the night. The next day I could see nothing of Hans and the *Irene* and tried to raise them on the VHF as we might have been very close. They were on their way to Cape Town, so we should be holding the same sort of course for the first couple of weeks and would probably see each other again.

DAY SEVEN: WEDNESDAY 17 FEBRUARY 1988

The second day was clear and blue but the next was overcast. The seas have been fine with a steady wind. The barometer is extremely high for this region: 1021 and steady. I don't mind this. My position is 45° 00′S 44° 09′W. I am close to where the large iceberg was sighted by the Navy last week, and worrying about whether I should sleep at night or stay on watch. The weather gets warmer the further north I am. I've had northerly winds since leaving and have been hard on the wind going north-east. I spoke to Hans and Lydia on the VHF and discovered that we have been only twenty miles apart for the last two days, which is incredible after seven days at sea.

The winds failed yesterday evening, and for most of the night I was either becalmed or going along very slowly. The wind came round to the south-east and then gradually to the east. I could still make north-east, but later it came north of east and I'm going north. Oh well, that's life.

This morning I tried to get the generator going but it kept stopping. I thoroughly checked the carburettor and then started her up. She ran beautifully when outside her box, but as soon as I put her back in I got a hell of a shock, even wearing rubber gloves – perhaps they were damp. Most things are. The Army hadn't managed to find the fault and the problem is driving me slightly round the twist. I can't use power tools without it. I'll have another go and rebuild the whole thing using the old engine.

I had to stop working. I was exhausted and had bad pains in my chest, probably caused by starting the Mase a couple of days ago to charge the batteries. I find the pull-start really exhausting, especially when I have to make several attempts. I might have to carry on using the engine until I get the Mase sorted out. When there is more sunshine on the solar panels things will ease a bit. Lately it's been overcast most of the time.

DAY ELEVEN: 21 FEBRUARY 1988

I've just filmed some whales. I glanced out of the main hatch and saw something like a mast sticking up out of the water and then lying horizontally. It was about half a mile behind the boat and I thought it was a boat without sails in distress, rolling violently. I watched for

157

a few moments and then another appeared, the fin of a whale sticking right up in the air. I quickly got out the camera and filmed for about ten minutes. I've got big whales, small whales, and some sea in between. The camera got rather wet so I dried it and put it away. Today's run was 120 miles.

I'm back in touch with Alistair on the Durban net, and his helper in Cape Town who takes my positions daily. *Irene* is still very close, within twenty miles.

DAY THIRTEEN

Today's run has been ten miles so far. I was becalmed for the best part of yesterday, rolling around with sails banging, but in spite of that a warm sunny day. It was a pity there wasn't enough breeze to hold everything tight and keep her moving. Now the wind has come up and she's away, doing around 6 knots. Maybe today won't be so bad after all.

DAY FIFTEEN

Sighted Hans on the horizon but he couldn't have spotted me as there was no response on the VHF. I made some bread. I ate nothing but bread. Big sandwiches. It was lovely.

DAY NINETEEN: MONDAY 29 FEBRUARY 1988

My position at 09.00 hours was 38° 40'S 29° 09'W. At last the wind is good, has gone round to the north and I'm managing to make a north-east heading. I had to run the engine this morning as the batteries were nearly flat; I could hardly get through on the radio. There are still problems with the Mase, but my chest has hurt so much since last week that I shall put off starting it until I feel better.

My staysail is ripped at the foot which is pretty annoying. The material is rotting and my sails have had it. I'm a little concerned as I have still 8,000 miles to go. I might be able to make another out of a spare jib when I get to St Helena. The sails are held together with patches and glue: an extraordinary sight.

It's nearly 2,000 miles to St Helena and another 300 to Cape Town. I might consider going in there if things get seriously out of hand. I could buy some new sails and have a few beers. My intention was to plod on to St Helena if possible, make repairs or wait until the sails can be sent in by ship. I'll have to think about it.

Hans on *Irene* is still fairly close. We haven't been in contact today but I was twenty miles ahead of him yesterday. I've overtaken him, which is nice.

Most things on the boat seem to be working, apart from a few problems. This morning I motor-sailed for an hour while charging the batteries and everything seemed to be fine. I'll keep my fingers crossed. I must get out the needle, thread and glue at the first opportunity. I don't want to take the sail down at present as it's an uncomfortable sea.

DAY TWENTY-TWO: THURSDAY 3 MARCH 1988

There's a bit of a blow going on and the wind has gone round to the south-south-east, at about force seven with quite rough but beautifully blue seas. I filmed a bit this morning. Clouds come and go and it's fine in between. Not bad at all and reasonably warm.

This morning I heard on the Durban net that the South Atlantic high is below me. It must have been the Horse Latitudes that I came through when I was becalmed last week. The high pressure is pretty far south at the moment. Maybe I can battle my way far enough east to get into the south-east trades.

Kay Cottee, the Australian yachtswoman who is making a non-stop circumnavigation on her boat, *First Lady*, was behind me coming around Cape Horn, and overtook me while I was in the Falklands. I haven't been in touch with her but have had various messages about her progress. The crew on the *Worra* took mail out to her as she was coming past Stanley. She is now on her way south. I've got her position and our paths are going to cross somewhere. We might even see each other, which is something to look forward to.

I have been in contact with Mike Francis, a radio ham in St Helena, to ask him if he thought I could use a fisherman's mooring, and save myself having to anchor. He seemed to think that that would be in order, and offered to have a word with the dock foreman. I've now got quite a few radio contacts going around the world, am in touch with the Falklands every night and Jean in Wales each morning. She gave me a message from Chris Rudd asking whether I would be interested in doing a circumnavigation with a disabled crew. I told him I'd have to think about it. Thought about it for ten seconds and said yes.

I have finally got the sail off and the small spare jib up. It's not as efficient as the staysail but seems to be doing quite nicely. The sail is bagged and I intend to leave it like that until I reach St Helena and find out what can be done there. I might be able to stick some material around the edges, to reinforce them sufficiently to get me home. There is patch upon patch on both the staysail and jib.

DAY TWENTY-EIGHT: WEDNESDAY 9 MARCH 1988

My position is 28° 55'S 20° 31'W. I was becalmed not only last night, but the previous day and the night before: about thirty-six hours in all. This morning a slight wind came up from the south-west, which was terrific, and I set all sails. I then decided to repair the fluxgate compass which had gone wrong a few days earlier. Either the connections were faulty or the wires disconnected in the wiring loom. I cut out a length of wire and rejoined it by twist-jointing. The contact wasn't very good, so while it was calm this morning I soldered it, working just inside the main hatch, out of the breeze. I'm glad to have that job out of the way; it is rather difficult steering by the sun and stars. After a cup of coffee I thought about tackling the Mase which still cuts out after a few minutes. I have checked everything in the fuel department and had the carburettor to pieces more often than I can remember. I don't know what is wrong, but think it must be the coil breaking down under the load. I may rebuild it using both the old Mase engine and the new alternator.

I motor-sailed for about an hour in a light wind. She was doing 5 knots and more as the wind increased. I switched the engine off and put the jib away, as it was shielded by the main and staysail. Ten minutes later she started careering off course and I couldn't control her by steering. I put one reef in the main which wasn't enough so in a wind which had increased to full gale force eight, I tried putting in the next two reefs. The sail was pinned up against the mast and the batons caught around the shrouds. I was careering along and it took half an hour's hard work to get the mainsail down. It is at last lashed to the boom, which I let drop down, and secured to the rails. There was little enough time to act. Luckily the downhaul was on top of the main, enabling me to put it on the winch and tug it down. Even if I had broken the batons or damaged the sail, at least she was safe.

I've been running for about three hours on a third of the staysail, at about 4 knots with the wind on the quarter. There is a real old gale blowing out there but it is better than being becalmed. It's only about 400 miles before I reach the Trade Winds, which will take me the 1,100 to St Helena. At least, that's the idea. Twenty-eight days from the Falklands to where I am now. My plan was forty days, so maybe, with a bit of luck, I'll do it.

DAY THIRTY-THREE: MONDAY 14 MARCH 1988

Today's position at noon was 24° 12'S 15° 22'W. I was running on the engine for three hours yesterday and will do the same today. I've been averaging only 1–2 knots in very light winds for the past two days and can only make east which is alright as I need a bit of east, but is dreadfully slow. Yesterday I did only forty miles. The Horse Latitudes must have come back up north. I expected this. Last night the log clocked up another 10,000 miles, making 30,000 in all: quite a fair chunk.

Triumph! I have now rebuilt the Mase generator as planned, using the old engine. Halfway through the job I discovered why it was cutting out. When the Army tried to repair it they didn't replace the insulation on the stop wire which occasionally earths out. When it was back together again there were no more electric shocks. It must have been the coil. I can now start it without wearing rubber gloves. I've used it three times and been quite extravagant with battery power, which is a treat. Recently the log showed only 4 knots during a time when I was averaging 5, which gives an idea of how slow the log is.

A cardboard box has floated by. The best thing I've seen for ages.

I heard this morning that the mooring fee is going up in St Helena. It will be doubled on 1 April, making it £32. That is rather expensive as there are no facilities, no harbour, and one has to anchor.

DAY THIRTY-SIX: THURSDAY 17 MARCH 1988

My position is 22° 33'S 13° 04'W. It's one of those bloody awful days. I've been kicking and swearing. For the last three days there has been no wind at all, and this morning it's from the north-east which is

161

where I want to go. It's so light a wind I can steer only north or south-east. I ran the engine yesterday for five hours, and last night the wind came up very light from the south-east. I was able to sail at about 2 knots in the right direction. This morning has been hot with clouds and rain, the clouds going one way and the wind another. I'm heading north at 0.2 knots, which seems to be the pace. If I ever get up to three knots again, I'll be so excited that I'll probably go straight out and reef in the sails. Oh dear.

I've made some bread and cleaned the cooker.

I can't go faster than 4 knots on the engine for some unknown reason. I wonder if the propeller has barnacles growing all over it and is cavitating, making air bubbles that explode and burn the propeller. I tried the pitch in several different positions, but it didn't help.

At ten o'clock this morning I was 643 miles from St Helena. I'm getting there. I had hoped to be there by next week. I suppose I could still do it if the wind comes up, but it's unlikely. I must have crossed Kay Cottee's track by now but haven't seen her: a pity.

DAY FORTY: MONDAY 21 MARCH 1988

The day I thought I would reach St Helena. One can't be right all the time. I've had good winds for the last twenty-four hours, but coming from the north-east. I've been able to make east, but want to go where the wind is coming from. At least I've had some wind and have been able to move along a bit. I only hope I find the Trade Winds shortly.

I have not wasted time but repaired the Autohelm which was quite an undertaking. The wires to the brushes in the motor are as fine as human hair. One had corroded and a brush broken. I don't know whether it happened when I took it to pieces. The brush is only a quarter of an inch by an eighth, with a hole in one end on which it pivots. It is held on by a minute clip, and the brush was broken on the pivot point. I glued it and left it to set for a day while I cleaned up the rest of the Autohelm which needed a bit of attention. Yesterday I put it together again. Working with a soldering iron is quite difficult on a rolling boat as even the slightest movement distracts one's eye. I managed with my specs and a magnifying glass, trying to keep myself steady.

Next I set about the sewing machine, putting in the two condensers that the Army had given me. They were not the right type but I thought they might work and although they do, it is impossible to switch off the motor, which runs all the time. I took the foot switch to pieces and found a leaking condenser which could have been shorting the switching mechanism. Taking that out, I tried another, but the result was the same. I should be able to get her working if I can get some condensers in St Helena. For the time being I could fix an on/off switch and operate it with my foot. Yes. Perhaps that would work.

DAY FORTY-TWO

Time to do some carpentry. The deck head outside the loo needs finishing. Sawing a piece of plywood to the correct size, I screwed it up in place, but hit a wire and fused the lights. I then had to find exactly where the wire was broken, and the job turned into a slightly bigger one. Perhaps I'll carry on and put the door on the loo. I'd like to fit it out and finish the panelling. I have some mosaic for the floor but need glue, which I'll try to get in St Helena. Once started I want to carry on. It's getting started that's the problem.

The wind is lightening and it will soon be evening. I hope its strength and direction improve as I could do with a break, having done only 350 miles in the last seven days. It's not very good. It will be nice to get ashore again, have a few beers and make some phone calls.

DAY FORTY-FOUR: FRIDAY 25 MARCH 1988

My position is 20° 23′S 8° 23′W. A bit of wind today but from the north-east. Three hundred miles to go and I'm exhausted. I seem to have spent most of the time becalmed or in light north-easterly winds, doing about fifty miles a day and trying to make east.

I got down to some more work around the boat. I built the frame, finally hung the door on the loo and finished varnishing it this morning. A good job done. I checked the battery and the engine water, which had a leak on the pipe. I ran the engine and she boiled, the raw water pipe twisted and flattened, stopping the water supply. Adjusting the belts, I went to clean the diesel filter, and found it still clean. Sod's Law. I thought it might be wise to check it before going into harbour so that the engine doesn't stop again. I switched on the Autohelm and found that it worked in reverse, steering backwards. I don't know

163

how I managed it. There is a switch to pull inside which will operate it in either direction, so I put that back in the right position. It's now working fine. And then I replaced the wires on the anchor winch.

I have a radio net working in the Falklands and sometimes contact with Chuck and Harry in Canada who come on the frequency in the middle of the night. I set my alarm and get up for them, but haven't been able to get through recently. Contact with Jean has also been poor but I can pass my position on through Ros in Cape Town.

I have been swearing a great deal for the last few days. I don't know which is worse, wind in the wrong direction or no wind at all. Probably no wind. I was becalmed for the whole of last night, sails and boom banging about. I lashed everything down as hard as I could, but things still crashed around. I am not using the navigation lights at night but a gas lamp on deck instead, which shines out brightly and saves a bit of battery power.

I need someone to talk to. Three hundred miles to go, which would take only about eight hours by car. Even if I wanted to use the engine to motor-sail it would be the best part of three days. I'll settle for the wind and hope to steer a better course. Maybe I'll try the other tack later today. I'll just have to see.

DAY FORTY-SIX: 27 MARCH 1988

I've a south-easterly wind which came up this morning. It made two or three attempts but disappeared and I was left wallowing again. Then it started slowly, gradually getting better and better and I'm now holding a course for St Helena at between 3 and 4 knots for most of the time. There are lulls still, but she hasn't stopped. It's terrific. Now only 250 miles to go, so I should be there the day after tomorrow. I'll try to get the dinghy out and inflate it and get everything ready. I'd better run the engine to make sure it hasn't got an airlock after the cleaning of the filter.

The boat was pointing so badly yesterday that I thought I'd better repair the foot of the sail. I stuck it together with rubberized carpet glue, patched it and attached a strip of cloth along the foot as reinforcement; this also stops the sunlight rotting the fabric underneath. I had another look at the sewing machine, hoping to be able to use it again, but once switched on I could only stop it running by taking out the plug. Unless I do this very quickly, it careers all over the cloth. As it happened I didn't need it as the wind had freed off and I made a sensible course on the sails already up.

The Sailomat is groaning – a worrying sound. I had greased it in Stanley and again the other day. I can't understand what the problem is, but it might not be serious. I'll have a look while I'm in St Helena. On my arrival there my circumnavigation will be complete. I shall cross my outward track in St Helena. I'm looking forward to that.

DAY FORTY-EIGHT

Forty-five miles off St Helena and it's just getting dark. I should be there in the morning. I had hoped to see the island tonight but it is misty. I keep imagining that I'm seeing land. I'll have to judge my speed and course to get there. It's tight, as I've been hard on the wind for the last few days trying to make a course, and at one time thought I was going to miss by about forty miles. I think I'll just about make it, but won't know until daylight tomorrow.

I had some good contacts on the radio today. I listened to Jean talking to Ros in Cape Town and could hear her quite well, although they couldn't hear me. I heard Jean say that Bob wanted me to ring him at HTV on Thursday. I should have a few beers inside me by then, but I'll do my best. I also spoke to another yacht through the Durban net: a man from Johannesburg. He sailed with his family to St Helena, arriving yesterday, and said that I could call him on the VHF in the morning and he'll be there to help me pick up a mooring. It's nice to know there's somebody listening out for me and there's a bit of help waiting in the harbour.

It's been hard going the last few days. First of all no wind, then having to scrape a course and getting too close in to the shore during the night. I have slowed down, probably too much, but it's difficult to judge. I don't want to run into the island during the night, and the chances of seeing it are pretty remote. There is a moon but it sets early. I'm quite excited about getting in.

My landfall at dawn was good. The outline of the island appeared in the grey sky when I was about ten miles offshore. The wind started to go around to head me as I got closer, and four miles off Jamestown I switched on the engine and motored in. I could see the Royal Mail

165

ship, *St Helena*, at anchor in the bay, and a small dinghy with the tall man I'd talked to waiting to help me.

Soon I was ashore and meeting old friends. I spent most of the first day sitting in the shade at the café, Ann's Place, with a cool beer in my hand. I rang Bob, who gave me the good news that he and Gillian were flying to Horta and would be there on 4 July.

Once again I stayed with Doug, as I had on my outward passage, and was able to use his sewing machine to mend the sails. We went fishing, taking our catch of tropical fish back to his canning factory, where he tinned and labelled it for me to bring home.

The local radio station asked me for an interview and told me I was the first yachtsman to make a circumnavigation from St Helena. I was delighted as I hadn't realized that it was apparently rather difficult to do. It made all those days struggling to zero zero, then against the Trades and finally across the Horse Latitudes, worthwhile.

The Governor of St Helena's many friends in the Falklands had sent him many messages. Hearing that he had finished his term of office and was leaving the island, I thought he would be too busy to see me. As he left, I was on the quay watching as he walked down the line of smartly dressed dignitaries, shaking their hands and chatting to them. On an impulse I stood at the end of the line, put out my hand to shake his and told him of meeting his friends. He seemed delighted, having heard a radio interview about my voyage the previous night. We talked for about a quarter of an hour, me in jeans, tee shirt and flip-flops and the rest of the line in suits, collars and ties, looking most uncomfortable in the hot sun.

One day I was sitting on the landing steps, watching the local fishermen unload their catch, when I saw a familiar face being rowed ashore in a dinghy. When he landed we looked at each other wondering where we had met before. It had been in Cape Town on my outward passage. He was Ed Bryant, an American, who makes his living as a yacht delivery skipper. When he heard that I had just sailed up from the Horn he told me that, although he'd been sailing for twenty years and covered many thousands of miles, that was an experience he had yet to have. On my birthday he climbed to the top of the mast to repair my VHF aerial and I asked him and his crew to join me for dinner at Ann's Place. He would have liked that, but had already embarked on the evening's cooking and invited me to join him. Some hours later he came across, wondering whether he could bring the food over to me instead, having asked an extra couple from another yacht and realized that he wasn't going to have enough room. Twenty-one people turned up. Ed had been quietly organizing a surprise party. Someone had made a birthday cake with about 250 candles on it and everyone brought presents and drink.

Lots of people turned out to help as I left St Helena. Ed's crew carried my stores down to the boat and rowed it all out for me. He and several others helped cast me off, but once again the propeller kept on jamming in reverse. I dared not adjust it then, but turned the boat through 180° to leave the mooring and, I hoped, sail off between the other boats. We cast off the bow, I put one of the headsails out, the boat swung round 90° and we let go of the stern. She should have carried on around the other 90°, but didn't, instead sailing straight for a rather classy fibreglass yacht, the *Moojardi*. Luckily there were enough of us on board to fend her off, helped by the owner of the threatened boat. I spoke to him later on the radio and he said that everything was fine, although I had nearly given him a million-dollar heart attack. Once clear, everyone got into Ed's dinghy to be rowed ashore and I sailed off for Ascension.

The next 700-mile leg was incredibly easy, as after Day Two I had no need to touch the sails. It was exceedingly pleasant sailing along doing nothing, just sitting in the sun enjoying it all. I could have made a quicker passage but was not in a hurry until I ran out of Scotch.

I keep on getting messages from John Osborne, asking me for an estimated time of arrival. He wrote to the Falklands saying he might sail out to meet me. Does he mean the Azores or Cardigan Bay? I don't know.

I hope I can manage to get into Ascension and drop anchor with the propeller in its present state. And after that, if I have to go into the Azores with only forward drive, manoeuvering would be very difficult. There are rather too many expensive yachts in marinas these days: another problem to resolve.

So far I've tackled only one job. Yesterday I repaired the two solar panels, having to solder some bad joints together. The repair lasted for only twenty-four hours, when they stopped working once again, so I'll have to re-do it. The compass needs repairing too, as the soldered joints are inadequate. I might ask the Navy to do it for me while I'm ashore. I could beach the boat and do some work on the propeller and

167

everything else that needs doing. I'll decide in the next couple of days.

A message came via the Durban net to say that anchoring at Ascension was quite easy. My main worry was being unable to reverse or turn in a tight angle. But it turned out to be an open anchorage and I was able to go straight in. I dropped sails when half a mile off the beach and motored. There were a lot of barges and some small boats on moorings. While going in, I noticed a water jet boat zooming around, photographing me. I waved to him. He waved back and continued taking photographs. 'What have I done now?' I wondered to myself.

I dropped anchor in a nice open spot about 400 yards from the beach and switched off the engine. The wind was quite strong, she drifted back and the anchor bit.

12

Last Leg

The jet boat came alongside and the pilot introduced himself as David Warrin, the captain of the *Maersk Ascension*, a large blue tanker anchored a mile offshore. He wanted to know if there was anything he could do to help, having been asked by the Ministry of Defence to look after me. I wondered whether I could have a shower aboard their ship and was told that I could, and a cabin to go with it. I said that I'd better stay with the boat until I was sure the anchor had taken, and put out the rest of the chain, 150 feet. The longer the chain, the better the holding. Getting my gear together, I went out to the tanker in the jet boat.

Once alongside I saw to my horror a boarding ladder slung over the side with a climb of thirty feet above the water in store for me. There was a large swell and we had to grab the ladder as the jet boat rose on a wave up the side of the ship, jump on to it and climb. By the time I reached the top, I was gasping for air and had to sit on a bollard for about five minutes to get my breath back. It was worse than usual, as I hadn't been walking at all for a week.

David and I strolled a hundred yards to the main superstructure. It was quite a big tanker, almost 60,000 tons. Up more stairs and he took me into the bar for a couple of beers, by then it was dinner time and the best meal I'd had for weeks. After that David showed me to the pilot's cabin with its shower, double berth, and desk. I was told to make myself at home and sleep on board if I wanted to. He told me that the night watch would keep an eye on my boat and, if the worst came to the worst, the anchor dragged and she drifted out to sea, they would go and find her in the morning.

I had a shower, went back to the bar and met some people who had come aboard for drinks including David the Spy, so called because he worked for GCHQ at Cheltenham, who have radio listening posts out here. It became quite a party, and as the evening wore on I got my second wind. All I had wanted earlier was to get some sleep as I hadn't had much the night before.

The next day we went back to the boat to make sure it was alright, and took the solar panels, compass and radar detector back to the *Maersk* to be repaired. Later David took me ashore to see the police. It's not a very welcoming island, as you are allowed only a forty-eight-hour stay. I asked if it would be possible to extend this to five days and was told to come back the following day to see the chief of police. David took me to look around the island. We met some Air Force officers and their wives and went with them to the Red Lion pub at the top of Green Mountain, afterwards visiting the Administrator who lives in a lovely house perched on a plateau halfway up the mountain. It was rather like a trek up the Burma Road. Once there I asked him if I could have a piece of bamboo, which grows on the heights, to use as a spinnaker pole. He very kindly agreed and said that he would ask the government farm to organize it. I also asked one of the Air Force officers if they would find me a morse key, so that I could practise. They found one which was almost antique.

Back to the boat for dinner and another night in the bar. I went ashore the next day to meet the chief of police who refused to let me stay, until I told him that the crew of the *Maersk Ascension* were repairing some of my things, one of which was the compass. He agreed that I couldn't sail without it and gave me leave to stay for the five days I had wanted.

I was taken out to parties every night, but if I wanted to stay ashore after seven o'clock had to find an islander to sponsor and stay with me. Although it is part of the United Kingdom they take one's passport away, something I wouldn't dream of giving up in any other part of the world.

The radio officer from the tanker mended the solar panels and got the radar detector working. He was about to repair my compass and asked the Air Force for some special wire to do it with. Instead, they sent over some lads to do the job. Unfortunately they couldn't fix it and I rather wished the radio officer had been left to get on with it.

I was on the *Maersk* for ten days and when I left was given duty-free stores. I could have had as much diesel as I wanted, and it was a pity that I'd filled the tanks in St Helena. They gave me petrol, a lot of food, five cases of beer, three bottles of whisky, three of gin and a bottle of rum: enough to keep me going for a while.

When I set sail for the Azores they all came to see me off and I showed David how to operate the video camera. I pulled up the anchor while the jet boat held me in place so that it was not necessary to use the engine. When the anchor was up and stowed, I went back to the cockpit and the jet boat cast me off. I put up the mainsail and sailed between some barges and smaller boats and past the *Maersk*. David did a grand job of filming me putting up the sails and sailing past the tanker, waving to the crew on board. They brought the boat alongside and handed back the camera and that was that. I was on my own again and off once more.

DAY THREE

Beautiful sailing since I left; 120 miles on the first day and 130 yesterday and today. It's very hot, but not too bad as there's a bit of a breeze, a dead following wind which is coming into the cabin. At first I was on a broad reach, making it pretty hot in the boat, and I hope the wind keeps up for a while. If so I might be in the Azores earlier than I expected. I've allowed myself enough time to be becalmed for quite long periods so I'm almost certain to have good sailing all the way.

DAY SEVEN: 18 MAY 1988

My position is 2° 22′N 20° 50′W. A good day's sailing on Sunday, and on Monday I crossed the Equator. It was a thoroughly nasty day, the first ugly-looking sky I've had for a long time: Doldrums stuff, streaks and mares' tails. I managed to sail on course all day, but during the night was becalmed for quite long periods in between squalls. This time I didn't have much of a celebration, I must be becoming blasé.

I'd intended to have tea and cucumber sandwiches on deck but instead had them in the shade of the cabin. Much cooler. Dolphins were playing around the boat.

I mended the solar panels yet again, finding another bad joint, and filmed myself taking them off and repairing them. I can get 2 amps from the two panels but if one of them doesn't work, neither does the other. Yesterday the winds were very light, force two, and I managed sixty miles, sailing rather slowly. I charged the batteries with the Mase as the sky was too cloudy for the panels.

A wide blue sky with just one black cloud following me, which every now and then catches up, blown by the wind: the only time I do any real sailing. As soon as I get away from it, the wind drops, the cloud catches up again and so it goes on. Very slow going.

I motored for a couple of hours to try and find a little puff of wind to cheer myself up. It is so hot that I'm pouring with sweat: the engine is running and there's heat from that as well. It's going to be a hot night. If there's a little breeze I can at least sit in it and feel cooler. In the evening I go on deck and sling buckets of water over myself, then have a fresh water shower with the crop sprayer. I can't do it too often, as I must ration the water.

I found a leak on the foot pump supplying the fresh water tap, which leaks every time I use the sink. If the worst comes to the worst I could take the pump off and move it into the sink so that it can be used at the highest point.

I had a good radio contact with Jean in Anglesey and later talked to Hugh Gibbs in the Azores. He lives near Horta and we are looking forward to meeting each other. I told him that I've a bit of a problem, as I'm unable to reverse, and might need help getting into the marina. It is good to know that there is somebody on shore to give me a hand. I hope soon to have news of other boats that I've come across who have gone on ahead to the Azores.

I shall have a gin. I'm drinking far too much, it's the bloody heat. At least I suppose it is. On the way out, and also on my first voyage, I was less affected by it but now it's really getting to me, probably because I haven't been to the tropics for a while. I spent a lot of time in the Southern Oceans, New Zealand and the Falklands, and it wasn't until I was halfway to St Helena that it started to get really warm. I'm doing half a knot, and not a bad direction either, north-eastish according to the sun, just about right. I hope I can keep going; at least when I'm sailing there's no noise of slatting sails and a crashing boom. My position: 02° 22′N 20° 50′W.

DAY THIRTEEN: TUESDAY 24 MAY 1988

I've had thunder, lightning and squalls in the night, followed by days of being becalmed and slow progress. In spite of that on most days I've made a reasonable distance, the worst being fifty-eight miles. It's been very hot, and for the last week the wind has come from the north. I've been going very slowly towards the north-west and last night tacked back to the east. I didn't gain anything, but it made a change.

I have a heat rash, a bit of a problem as if I wash in sea water it may well turn into salt water sores. I haven't enough fresh water and just hope that the weather cools off a little in the next few days. This morning when the sun came up it was 80°F in the cabin and it's very oppressive. There have been a few days with heavy cloud cover which caused a damp heat.

As the pump is leaking, I have to keep the kettle filled so that I don't lose water each time I use the tap. This stops the floor getting constantly wet. The solar panels are working quite well when there's no cloud. The boat doesn't seem to be pulling as well as she used to – probably the sails are getting stretched, they've been patched so much. I haven't had the propeller fully feathered for about four days, but left it in the motoring position in case I met a ship. This morning I moved it back, the speed picked up a half a knot straight away and she pointed higher to the wind, which has helped my course. When I have to use it again I only hope I can find forward drive.

DAY FIFTEEN: THURSDAY 26 MAY 1988

My position is 08° 45′N 26° 27′W. Yesterday a bulk carrier came over the horizon. I watched her anxiously as she was on a collision course with me. It was just after daybreak, too late to have the navigation lights on and not very good visibility. I called them on the radio but there was no reply. She came closer and I tried again. Still no reply. Getting out the searchlight I shone it at the bridge but there was no response. I started the engine and after several attempts found forward drive and motored ahead. She then changed course to port and passed close astern of me. Once more I tried to make radio contact without success. Within half an hour another carrier appeared who also would not answer me. They must be on course for South America. It is maddening when they make no attempt to say that they've seen one. I ran the engine again for a few minutes and left it in drive. Although it slows me down, at least if I see another ship I can motor without delay. As my radar detector didn't go off I think they can't have had theirs going. I looked through the binoculars but couldn't see scanners going round.

A short while ago the wind went around and I'm making a better course, a slightly better course. I went to put out more of the jib and found two ripped seams. It's too windy to take it down now and might make things worse, so I'll leave it for the time being. It will be yet another thing to slow me down, as I've only about four feet of sail out, hardly worth having. However, I have left plenty of time to get to the Azores and I'm doing my best. My average since leaving Ascension is 3.4 knots, and I've only 1,760 miles to go. Not too bad for fifteen days, taking into account that I've been through the Doldrums. I hope the wind goes round a bit and gives me an easier time.

DAY SIXTEEN: FRIDAY 27 MAY 1988

I cut my hair, taking six inches off the back, which was quite a feat. I parted it in the middle, took one half from the back, held it in my mouth and felt for my ear lobe with the scissors. With one cut it was done. I repeated the operation on the other side. I don't know what it will look like by the time I get to the Azores. It looks a bit strange now.

DAY TWENTY

The main halyard winch is very stiff. Something had gone radically wrong inside so I took it to pieces. I can't put the main up without it and decided to take it off and swap it for the sheet winch on the weather side, which I'm not using. Luckily I was able to undo the screws, which hadn't been touched for three years, and overhauled it, finding that a couple of teeth had broken off, fallen into the works and jammed everything.

DAY TWENTY-ONE

There were strong winds of force seven during the night, and when I looked out in the morning a halyard was hanging loose from the staysail. Either the block had broken or the shackle had come undone. I couldn't unfurl the sail as the halyard would have gone round with it, and had to think of a way of getting it and the block back up the mast again. I used the spare to pull the block, with the staysail halyard threaded through it, up the mast to above the staysail. It took quite a few hours to get it organized but now at least I can furl the sail. I was running short on sails. Luckily the winds were light, making it possible for me to do the job.

There is a lot of red Sirocco dust on board which has come nearly 2,000 miles across the sea from the coast of Africa. There is thick dust on the rails, and when I took the sail down today the halyard was covered as well. There must be even more at the top of the mast, and I hope the navigation light is visible.

DAY TWENTY-THREE: 3 JUNE 1988

The first day that conditions have been quiet enough for me to take the sail down. The splits in the seams aren't very long, so it's a sewing by hand, glue and patches job. I don't think there is any major damage to the sail.

Today I mounted the camera outside. The plate where the mounting screws into the camera has been giving me a bit of a problem. I had to glue it in because the camera was flopping about. It's time I did some of the filming of myself working that I promised Bob.

DAY TWENTY-FOUR

Today I started the Mase and charged the batteries. After lunch I was having a little siesta when I heard what sounded like a rifle shot. I went up on deck to find the aft lower shroud had broken at the base. I reefed down to take a bit of the loading off the mast, and set to work. Unfortunately there was no time to set up the camera. I had to get it done quickly, managing to shorten the cable three inches. I remade the compression joint, and in two hours had it all back together again and tensioned. I left the sail well reefed down as I couldn't have stood

175

another bang in the night. The mast is extremely vulnerable when that happens. The shrouds shake about like mad things if the tension is taken off the weather side.

While I was trying to make the repair a pigeon landed on the rail and stood looking at me rather stupidly. I told him I would have a chat when I had finished. I was hoping he would fly away, remembering the sad fate of the last one. Eventually he took off in the general direction of the Cape Verde Islands, about 500 miles away to the east. There was quite a stiff wind blowing from that direction so he had a tough journey ahead.

I couldn't get the camera batteries charged in time to film, so repaired the sail, put it back up and finished the deck work. I got it all done by nightfall and we are back in fair shape again. It was beginning to look quite dramatic with a torn jib and broken halyard block but it's all sorted out now and I'm going to have a beer.

DAY TWENTY-FIVE

I had some time off after all the hard work and then started on some carpentry, finishing the steps down to the fore-cabin, so that the paint tins underneath can no longer be seen – much tidier. I still have to varnish the wood but am waiting until later. As I finished a bosun bird tried to land on the antenna at the top of the mast. I think they are also known as tropic birds.

The wind is still north-north-east and fairly light. I'm struggling to make a course and the current is taking me to the west. When I'm going slowly it has quite an effect on the westerly drift, between 1 and 2 knots. Sargasso seaweed has started to build up, which is quite exciting. In the old days ships used to report gettting caught up in great floating islands of the stuff.

A message on the transatlantic net came through about a German yacht not too far away. It is a much bigger boat with a crew of ten and will overtake me in the next couple of days. No sign so far.

DAY TWENTY-SIX: 7 JUNE 1988

Gillian's birthday. I managed to get a message back to her via Jean to wish her a happy birthday. Jean recorded the message and then rang Gillian. A nice surprise for her. After that I built some shelves in the loo, at the end of the basin top. I've got the front of the cupboard at last and will put up a shelf to give me more storage space.

Last night there were squalls which woke me up. The wind was howling, rain was pouring down and I kept having to get out to reef and try to get her back on course. It was not very pleasant as I was under full sail, having gone to sleep in light winds. My course has improved a bit over the last few days but not as much as I'd have liked. At this stage I would prefer to be going north, not making any more west.

8 JUNE 1988

I haven't done a lot today. I got up late and then went back and slept again. I was tired after last night's storms, but cheered to find I've done 2,207 miles. Only 982 to go and an average speed of 3.3 knots: not too bad considering the bad winds there have been.

The log is not working properly. No matter what speed I'm doing, it won't go above 2 knots or record anything below 1.5 knots. It is very frustrating as it's encouraging to know how fast one is going and only too easy to start believing the log. I still have plenty of time to get to the Azores even if it's necessary to come back three or four hundred miles from the west. It's not too big a problem.

No more filming as yet. I might take some shots of the Sargasso weed which is forming windrows like hay in the sea.

DAY THIRTY-ONE: 12 JUNE 1988

I have been overtaken by a German yacht, a 16-metre sloop, *Walrus*. I didn't see her as they were a hundred miles to the east of me and having the same problems with their course. However she is going twice as fast, so the current can't have been affecting her so badly. Like me, however, they have been taken over to the west.

A few squalls, high winds and rain today which didn't last long, with the scuppers in the water for a while, followed by being becalmed. Terrible stuff after a fairly steady night. These squalls seem to come with the dawn.

Yesterday, I listened to the Trooping of the Colour on the radio. Then a Romanian ship, the *Mircesti*, went by without seeing me. I got on the VHF and the watch officer answered but still couldn't see

me. There was no danger, I was about two miles on his port beam, h
was going to miss me by miles. We chatted for a while. He was takin;
sugar from Cuba to Romania.

Another little drama early this morning: they always seem to happe
in the dark. I was getting up and heard a noise on deck. The staysa
had unfurled, the rivets had broken at the bottom, and the aluminiun
sections which lead into the drum had jumped out. I turned it aroun
by hand to furl it and lashed it up.

Jean called to ask me to keep a QSO with Tom Lewis in London a
the Science Museum, where he mans an amateur radio station ever
Sunday. He wanted to make contact with me and our conversatio
will be put out over loudspeakers in the museum.

I got back to the job in hand and took down the sail as it woul
have been pretty dangerous to leave it. Cutting the bent section out,
put it back in the drum and got the sail up again. Everything seeme
perfect. As I was setting it there was an enormous bang. The blood
stay had broken at the bottom by the bottle-screw. I furled it up an
lashed the sheets tightly as the stay was gyrating madly. If I an
becalmed again I shall be able to make that bottom joint good, but
will be a hell of a job. I did the last one in the cabin, clamping it wit
a vice to the side of the main hatch. This will have to be done on th
foredeck in a pretty steady sea or I'll never get the threads of the bottle
screw back together, and might do even more damage. I shall have t
sail to the Azores on the jib which is now taking the weight on th
front of the mast. I only hope the stay doesn't break. If that happene
I could lose the mast. After three years at sea things are beginning t
crack up. I must check it all over and do a lot of work when I'm nex
ashore.

I can hear the sound of humming. I wonder if it's caused b
submarines? The same thing used to happen in *Zane* II in this area
It's resonating through the boat. The sound has been coming an
going all afternoon.

DAY THIRTY-FIVE: 16 JUNE 1988

I sighted a tanker this morning, the *W.A. Mather*, registered in th
Isle of Man and heading astern to the north-east. I had a chat wit
the skipper, Stan Oakley, who had come from Mexico, making for th
Mediterranean.

It's been calmer today and I repaired the stay. I fixed a block to the base of the bottle-screw, using the electric winch to tension the stay, and started screwing it back together again. The sail is now up and I'm back in business. The only way in which I could have filmed myself working would have been to have the camera strapped up in the bow, where it might have been swamped with water. It was an emergency job and I couldn't waste time fiddling around with the camera.

DAY THIRTY-SIX

Fed up with going north-west yesterday, I decided to tack and head east for a day, but after about two hours the wind lightened until I was barely moving. In the morning I checked to see which way I was going. It was south, the wind was light and slightly west of north and it took me half an hour to get the boat turned round. It gradually came up and at last I am heading towards where I want to go, doing 3 knots. Incredible!

Some dorados were swimming around the boat: beautiful, nearly three feet long. In the water they are a lovely phosphorescent blue, but nearer the surface look bright gold. I started filming but the camera switched itself on and off, and when I looked through the eyepiece the image was jumping. I tried putting the battery in and out several times and it righted itself. The inside of the camera seems rather corroded. I'll have to do something about that in the Azores. I have some nice film of the dorados and the sunset but none of me working.

After I'd charged the batteries, I had a good contact with Hugh in the Azores, and then Jean who was shearing the sheep and couldn't stop to chat. My position is 32° 29′N 36° 57′W, and according to the Sat. Nav. there are only 548 miles to go, the qualifying distance required for the Ocean Yachtmaster's Certificate. A few years ago I took the first part, but didn't get round to the second as I hadn't clocked up enough sea miles.

DAY THIRTY-SEVEN: 18 JUNE 1988

I had a wonderful shower in the rain. It was great, suds everywhere, trying to keep the boat under control and getting soap in my eyes. Later, as I was once more becalmed, I decided to pack out the steering quadrant with shims, as there's a lot of play between it and the rudder stock. I needed calm weather, as once I had taken it off there would be no control over the rudder. The next task was to take the fresh water pump to pieces. I mended a small tear in the diaphragm with superglue after which it didn't leak any more.

DAY THIRTY-NINE: 20 JUNE 1988

I'm heading straight towards the North Atlantic high. Rudy, on the transatlantic net, had been giving me the positions of the isobars so that I could make a weather chart to plot the position and movements of the high. I can do nothing about avoiding it, absolutely nothing. I feel pretty desperate. At about 15.30 hours the wind from the southeast came out of nowhere and I'm doing about 1.5 knots. I eased the sheets, sailed on a course straight for Horta and by evening was only 400 miles away. I passed an orange buoy but couldn't get near it without tacking. These things never last for long, but I only managed forty miles, with the wind still from the east-south-east. In the evening I saw a shooting star or perhaps a satellite burning up: a marvellous sight.

DAY FORTY-ONE: 22 JUNE 1988

No wind this morning, nothing. And when it did come up it was from the north-north-west, a completely different ball game. I tacked off towards the east and sailed fifty miles in twenty-four hours.

DAY FORTY-THREE

I'm gradually getting the distance down. The wind is going round to the north-north-east, and trying to come back more to the east.

I tried to get through to Chuck in Canada but couldn't raise him and found myself talking to Eric in Wales. It was difficult but I could just make out what he was saying. He told me that Hans and Lydia on *Irene* had been shipwrecked off Agulhas. After setting off from Cape Town they were pitchpoled and consequently demasted. Happily they were rescued and are now safely back on land. Apparently they had suffered from the same thing as me, a broken steering quadrant.

My position is 35° 26′N 33° 41′W, and I'm heading towards the east. I wish I could bear round to the north, towards Horta again. It is seven days to the end of the month and another four before Bob and Gillian turn up. Eleven days in all. Not a great deal of time to spare.

I made some bread today and put all the ingredients together in the bowl, poured in the water but forgot to mix it. I kneaded it as usual, put it in the oven and it looks fine.

DAY FORTY-SEVEN

I receive BBC Radio Four quite clearly now and hear the shipping forecasts, but have lost contact with Hugh as I'm too close to land. We should be able to make contact again when I can see the islands. As I approach he is going to keep a lookout for me and drive to the harbour to help me in.

The wind has gone to the north-north-west and is getting stronger. The glass has dropped 10 millibars and it looks as though I shall be lucky and go in with a bit of a blow.

DAY FORTY-EIGHT: 29 JUNE 1988

Twenty-four miles and I still can't see land. On my previous voyage I could see Pico, a 13,000-foot volcano, from a distance of forty miles, but this time there is a lot of cloud and the island is hidden.

14.15 GMT

Land Ho! At last the eastern side of Pico has appeared through the mist. I've had to change course and come up harder to the wind. With full sail and the wind now at force six, she is bombing along.

Familiar landmarks started to appear and as I sailed along the side of the island I could see a light signalling from the hillside. I replied with my searchlight to Hugh flashing his car headlamps.

13

Going Home

I sailed to the harbour entrance, started the engine and motored in. Things have changed since I was last here, but Hugh had told me on the radio about the different layout. I could see people waving to me from the new customs quay, so I made a wide turn, switched off the engine, drifted upwind and stopped alongside the wall.

The customs men took the warps, made me fast and I stepped unsteadily ashore to shake hands with Hugh. As always, he was not what I had expected: people one has only talked to never look as you think they will. I had imagined Hugh would be large, heavy and dark, and instead he was short, light and fair. He had brought some friends to welcome me and they all came to the customs while I filled out the usual forms.

Late that evening I was enjoying a glass of Scotch when I heard someone jump off the quay, on to the deck and into the cockpit before I had got to my feet. Uninvited, a tall bearded man with a beaming smile planted himself on the seat in the pilot house and introduced himself as David Williams from Lampeter. He had come to see me while I was building *Zane Spray*. I remembered him. At the time he had been building a boat for eight years and I had almost caught him up after eight months' work on mine. He invited me to a meal on board, and I have to admit that he has done a beautiful job and, unlike mine, his is finished.

The new marina is excellent and for only £2 a day one can use water, electricity, showers and washing machines. Food and drinks in the town are very cheap, making Horta a good place to stay.

A few days later Hugh took me to the airport to meet Bob and Gillian. It was good to see her again after such a long time and we spent a very happy week in Horta. Bob wanted to take photographs of me sailing. The skipper of the Operation Raleigh brigantine, *Zebu*, towed me out of the berth using his dinghy, and with four of his crew we sailed over to Pico and back. Each time Bob wanted to take a picture the crew had to hide out of shot, and after he'd finished I told the youngsters that they could sail the boat for the next two hours while I served them sandwiches and beer.

There is a local tradition in Horta that visiting yachts paint their name on the harbour wall. Gillian and Bob came to see my inscription of *Zane* II and he offered to paint a picture of the *Zane Spray* and a chart of the voyage. Although the marina is only three years old, it is hard to find a space, but once we had, Bob spent the next few days wearing my straw hat and doing a good impression of Van Gogh.

Having travelled the last 4,000 miles with a broken compass, I was pleased that he had remembered to bring the spare part so that I could repair it. And waiting at the post office was the new radar alarm, which I had ordered to replace the old one which was no longer working. I was a little put out to discover that I owed 40 per cent import duty.

Jean had sent a letter and lovely photograph of herself. It is good to know what she looks like as I shall be meeting her for the first time when I return home. She said how much our radio contacts had helped her after the death of her husband. We have become very close over the last few months.

Soon after Gillian and Bob had flown home, Bill Gilmore, an American competitor in the single-handed transatlantic race, called to see me. He had been caught up in the same high pressure system as me and after a week of it had had enough, retired from the race and sailed into Horta. As we were both on our own we often had dinner together. He knew far more than me about the technique of sailing, but I could tell him of my experience of the seas in the Southern Oceans. I learnt a great deal from him at this late stage in my voyage.

On my last night ashore, I was invited on board a catamaran, *Let's Go*. The owner and two friends were taking the boat back to Britain after having left it in the Caribbean for a couple of years. I liked them a lot. Single-handed sailors make friends quickly. Perhaps if we didn't we wouldn't be able to spend so much time on our own.

I cast off the warps with Hugh and his friends to fend me off the other boats. Bill, who was also leaving, towed me out of my berth, but the wind carried me back to the marina before the boat was on a good enough course to start the engine. There was a flurry of panic in several languages and feverish fending off from the other boats before I was able to motor out of the harbour: another spectacular leave-taking!

Bill was heading for Gibraltar, going between St George and the northern coast of Pico. The wind was coming from the north, making it too tight for me to go that way. I could have done it but only by putting a tack in, and decided to go south of Pico, hoping to see him later. When I got to the south of the island the wind had gone round to the south-east, right on the nose. I had to tack. Then it changed and died altogether, leaving me too close to land. I motored until darkness fell and was becalmed off the east end of Pico for the night.

DAY THREE

On Day Two the wind came up and I sailed between the islands to Terceira, but by evening the wind had died and I was becalmed until the middle of the next morning. I was pretty frustrated. It was three days since I had left and I was still amongst the islands. I decided to motor for a while and after five and a half hours switched the engine off, to be completely becalmed again on a still, glassy sea. I took in all the sails apart from the main, to stop them crashing about. At three o'clock in the morning I woke up thinking that it was unusually quiet. I looked out and felt a light breeze coming from the south-west. I couldn't believe my luck. I winged out the main, got her on course and put out the headsails. I didn't pole out the staysail in case she gybed during the night, but went back to sleep.

When I woke up later the wind had increased and, still on course, I put out more sail. I've been going downwind ever since in a force four. I'm sailing as fast as I was going yesterday with the engine. Great stuff. I had been rather concerned because I didn't bother to fill up with diesel before leaving. There was room in the tank for only fifteen gallons or so, and it hadn't seemed worth sailing over to the fuel dock for that, and it was too far for me to carry it. However, I have now used about eight gallons motoring between the islands, and am beginning to think that I've not left enough time to sail home in seventeen days: HTV want me to arrive in Aberaeron on the evening of 12 August, during the week of the Yacht Club Regatta. I feared that I would be trapped in that high for several days. This wind was totally unexpected and at least I've got in one good day's sailing.

DAY FIVE

I can still see the outline of one of the islands on the horizon. Last night the wind went round to the north-west which was lovely and then gradually to north-north-east, where it has bloody well been ever since. I feel depressed and despondent and have tried every possible variation today, tacking this way, tacking that, but although the wind is strong it is right on the nose.

I had left myself twenty days to make the passage home from Horta. On my previous voyage it took me only thirteen. Here I am, on Day Five, only as far as I was in two, last time. I hope I'll make it. At the moment I'm heading east. I tried tacking to the north but she only wants to go west. I don't know what is wrong but it could be the sails. Yes, I'm sure the combination of the sails and the propeller pitch is making her better on one tack than the other.

The wind direction improved this afternoon but then worsened. I sailed sixty-eight miles but only made thirty miles headway on the chart. The Autohelm was broken and I tried to repair it, but failed. I'm afraid it's had it, so I motored for an hour and a half but had to steer the boat myself. A very light wind started to go round to the south-east, increasing to force two from the east. I started sailing again.

DAY SIX

I did ninety-two miles today: a distinct improvement. The barometer was at 1028 millibars, the wind up to force four and gradually force six. I was going about 6 knots, started the Mase, charged the batteries and had a good night's sailing.

DAY EIGHT: SUNDAY 31 JULY 1988

The wind went light again to the north-west and I thought that was the end of it but it went gradually north-north-west and the barometer kept falling, 10 millibars in twenty-four hours. Later the wind got up to force seven and I was still just about able to make my course. My day's run was 115 miles, and that evening I was passed by a merchant ship, the *El Dorado*. I asked them to switch on their radar so that I could check my new detector which they did. Moments later they came back asking whether I had any navigation aids on board. I told them that I have a Sat. Nav., thinking that they wanted to help me. However, they asked for my position as they had a problem with their system and wanted to know where they were. What an odd reversal of roles! I gave them a fix and wished them well.

Spotted another ship during the night, the *Oceanius*, a research vessel from the Woodhall Institute. I chatted with the master, who was interested in my voyage. Coming from Cape Cod, he knew all about Joshua Slocum. During our conversation he told me that one of their sister ships had discovered the wreck of the *Titanic*.

DAY NINE: 1 AUGUST 1988

Not doing too badly. The wind has gone round to the north, dropping from seven to five, and the barometer is coming up slowly. By evening the wind strengthened again. I reefed down well for the night, putting two in the main and using only half the staysail. Big waves and a strong sea.

I was up at three to make sure everything was alright, and by four one of the sails had started rustling in the wind. I thought something was wrong: it sounded like a loose sheet. The staysail was flapping. I tried to reef it in but the bottom of the alloy section had come out of the drum again, unfurling the sail which was flogging like mad. I let out the halyard a little to try and get it back, but was unsuccessful and decided to take the sail down. Fighting with the sail in the wind, I let go of the halyard, losing the end, which shot up into the air. I stood on top of the rails holding on to the shrouds and the end kept brushing my hand as I reached up into the darkness. The boat lurched and I almost lost hold, remembering that in the heat of the moment I hadn't clipped on my harness. I fell back on the deck and the halyard ran up through the block and landed on top of me. Exhausted, I stowed the sail neatly on the side deck, but didn't tie it. I was cold, wet, and pretty fed up by the time I got into the warm. I dried off and tried to sleep, but could hear a peculiar scratching noise under the boat. I went out once more to find the bloody sail had blown through the bow rails and gone under the keel. It was held only by the sheets, and the head of the sail was still on the stay. I dragged up a bit and sat on it, the waves coming over on top of me. Gradually, a little at a time, I pulled up more and sat on that until I got my breath back again. Eventually I had it all on the side deck and, as I should have done in the first place, lashed it to the side rails. I would have found the whole operation easier if I'd been in possession of two lungs, but in that case I suppose I wouldn't be here but farming in Wales. I dried myself again, made some coffee and waited for daylight.

DAY TEN: 2 AUGUST 1988

My position is 45° 24′N 17° 10′W. I've worn it down to 652 miles. I had a good QSO with Jean this morning, could hear her quite well and explained that I feel terribly under pressure about arriving on time. Things seem twice as bad when one's worried and I would so much like an easy sail home. I've been fighting my way around the world and could do without a deadline. I would just like this part of the voyage to be relaxed. I told her about the incident with the sail and halyard, not very good news. I'm now on a double-reefed main with only three feet of the jib out, all I can use because it is torn. There's no hope of getting it down in a force seven from the north. I have left the other sail lashed to the rails.

I've worked out how to repair the drum. It's a pity I hadn't thought of it before. As the sides of the drum are broken away, instead of relying on rivets, I will use a shackle with a jubilee clip going through it and then round the alloy section. That should hold it in place. The tape on the tack of the sail is broken, so the foot will have to be held in place with another jubilee clip.

I'm making east at 2.5 knots, on the mainsail only, praying that the wind will soon blow itself out and I can get back to a few repairs. To be able to mend the sails I need a lull in the wind and the seas to go down. As soon as that's finished, I'd like the wind to come up from the west at about force four for a few days.

187

DAY ELEVEN: 3 AUGUST 1988

The wind dropped enough last night for me to repair the furling gear. There's a block on the spare halyard at the top of the mast, so I used it to hoist the sail. First thing this morning, I got out on the foredeck with a rotary file and finished smoothing off the slot where the sail will feed in. I had to enlarge it. It was too small, as I had cut three inches off the alloy section. I got it all back together again and put the sail up. It was quite a struggle. Then I took a break and contacted Jean to tell her that the staysail was up and the jib down ready for repairing. Later I patched both sides of the jib and within an hour had it up. The sails might be up but I'm buggered, absolutely buggered, but happy to have it finished. I put the tools away, tidied the sheets in the cockpit and set her on a course heading north-west. The wind is still very light but could come back any time it wants to. I needed the lull and now I need the wind again. Will I ever be satisfied? My position is 45° 14′N 16° 25′W.

DAY TWELVE

It didn't come back but died away, and I sat there miserably. In the afternoon I motored for three hours. The evening forecast was south west force six, which would have been ideal. I went to sleep expecting to be wakened by a howling gale, but nothing happened until the morning when there was a faint little breeze from the south-west. It slowly strengthened until at eleven o'clock we started moving. I'm now goosewinged, going along at about 3 knots on a good course. The forecast is for a south-west force five, which would suit me fine.

Tomorrow I'll have a week in which to get there, 600 miles to do in seven days. I need some fair winds. I have to steer the boat when motoring, and lose my concentration after sitting at the wheel for three hours at a time. I'll plod on. I'm looking forward to getting home and seeing everyone, but it's not all plain sailing.

DAY THIRTEEN: 5 AUGUST 1988

I saw four fishing boats during the morning and later in the day lots of small trawlers. Two came quite close, passed astern and waved, one of the boats waving by numbers, the way they used to in the Navy

The crew stood in line and waved in time from side to side with their arms above their heads. It was quite comical, as though they were dancing. I don't know where they are from. Portugal perhaps. I'm not sure.

During the night I counted the lights of twenty boats around me. I could hear the engines but they were not very close. They were bombing up and down chasing fish, so I didn't sleep too well. My radar alarm woke me at about five o'clock: one of them was coming towards me but turned aside at the last minute and went in another direction. It was all quite exciting and I managed to sail all night goosewinged and poled out. I still haven't had to touch the sails and am making good headway.

Bad pains in my chest yesterday, probably from struggling with those sails. I know I did more than I am really capable of. The pain made me double up, it's like cramp in my chest which goes down my arms. It's pretty painful but it passes.

I put the Mase on this morning for a couple of hours and found I have enough two-stroke to last until I reach home. The diesel situation isn't too bad. After all, I've done only fifteen hours on the engine since leaving, thirteen of them while still within sight of the islands.

DAY FIFTEEN

I'm now about 380 miles from Aberaeron and 40 fewer from Fishguard. The sailing has been good. After losing sight of the fishing boats yesterday, I did 110 miles: a good run. And today, 80 miles in much lighter winds from the south.

I started the Mase to charge the batteries and heard a hell of a clatter. I thought I'd better look and see what was wrong, stripped it down and found that the rubber bushes had worn away. I replaced them with alkathene tube and she is running again. I'm trying to keep the batteries fully charged and leaving the Sat. Nav. on all the time because it's now more important to know exactly where I am.

I heard on the radio that a boat from Wales is heading for the Azores in the Ocean Cruising Club Race. He has just spent six days getting from Cardigan Bay to sixty-five miles south of Fastnet. Almost as bad as me.

The wind started coming up from the south-south-east, getting stronger all day until it reached force eight. I did 140 miles in twenty-four hours: a good run.

Concorde went over, the first time I'd heard it for three years. It's supersonic over the sea. I haven't heard anything so loud since the war, as if a bomb had fallen next door. After it had gone I slept for a bit and woke to find the sails backed and the pole bent in half. It's a write-off. Luckily I still have the bamboo pole from Ascension.

I haven't had good contacts for the past two days. I gave my position to the transatlantic net and my family will get it from them. This morning I managed to get through to Jean via Australia and told her that I had only 260 miles to go. She won't be on the air for the last two days of my voyage as she's going to Aberaeron to welcome me home. It will be good to meet her after having spoken to her for so long.

DAY SIXTEEN

Today is the eighth day of the eighth month, eighty-eight, and I was joined by killer whales who kept me close company for an hour. When I pumped the lavatory handle it squeaked and I heard them answer from underneath the boat. They seemed peaceful enough but it's good to know there is a steel hull between us, particularly as I'd just heard of a yacht being sunk by a school of them a few days ago.

It's now the evening and I'm pretty excited about arriving, it's quite a cliff-hanger. Two hundred miles to go and the winds are fairly light. It will take me two days to get to Fishguard where Bob wants to meet me. I think he would like to film my return to Aberaeron from *Zane Spray*. I must arrive there on Wednesday. Any later than that and I might as well carry straight on.

DAY SEVENTEEN

The wind is still holding, south-west force three, which couldn't be better. I'm making a straight approach to Small's Lighthouse. I've heard that Al from New Zealand will make contact at 07.30 hours tomorrow morning. I should be nearly in by then and hope I haven't got my hands too full to answer, as it would be nice to make contact with him for the last time on this voyage.

190

By evening I could see the loom of Small's Lighthouse on the starboard bow – an emotional moment: the first time I have seen Wales in nearly three years. I remembered those cold lonely days trying to fight my way out of Cardigan Bay and felt the first warmth of success.

I tried to sleep during the day but the excitement was too great. Later I met a fishing fleet and spent the first half of the night dodging them. I saw the last ferry heading for Fishguard and tried again to sleep.

The sun rose behind the Prescelly Mountains as the shore lights faded. At 07.30 I switched on the radio and called Al. His voice came back loud and clear to congratulate me from halfway round the world. I turned on the VHF to call the harbour authority and heard a yacht, *Moody Woman*, calling. Eric was on board a friend's boat waiting for my arrival in Fishguard.

As I sailed up to the harbour entrance the wind started to head me. I took down the sails and motored in to the still waters of the early morning. As I approached the anchorage and my chain rattled through the hawser, I could see Eric being rowed out.

I stayed quietly in Fishguard for two days and was made most welcome by the local people. There was a meeting in the Ship Inn with Bob and the HTV crew, to make final arrangements for my return on Friday evening. Neil the cameraman and Mike the sound engineer were to travel with me to Aberaeron so that they could film from the boat. Others would film from the shore. I asked John to join us to enjoy the last moments of my voyage.

At mid-morning on the 12 August 1988 we weighed anchor, raised the three-reefed main, gave her some headsails and sailed out of the harbour into a south-west force seven. *Zane Spray* took the bit between her teeth and headed for the last thirty miles home. The seas were large and following as she surfed down the waves. We ate sandwiches, drank beer, and laughed in the sunshine. The wind and the weather were kind.

We passed Aberporth and I remembered the rocket range incident with amusement. Then close to New Quay Head as we raced on home. I knew the weather was too rough for any of the local boats to come out to meet me but two miles off Aberaeron we saw spray ahead: Danny and Lloyd, risking all in their open fishing boat to escort me the last mile. It was difficult to hold back my tears as they motored alongside.

We took down the main, furled the jib for the last time and sailed into the entrance under half the staysail. John took the wheel from me. I stood on the side deck and saw the harbour walls lined with thousands of cheering people. We became shielded from the wind and the finishing cannon was fired. For a horrible moment I thought I'd been shot, which added to my joy when I realized I hadn't. I tried but failed to throw a line ashore and Danny and Lloyd came to the rescue. As I turned to wave to the crowd, there was such a roar of applause that you'd have thought I had scored a try for Wales at Cardiff Arms Park.

Friends pulled *Zane Spray* into the visitor's berth. Gillian, Gawaine and Jackie climbed down the ladder to greet me in the cabin. Sir Geraint handed me a magnum of champagne and welcomed me ashore. I walked through the crowd in a dreamlike state as people touched me and held my hands. My sisters, their children and friend's faces appeared in the crowd and then were swallowed up again. As I was pulled towards the yacht club I could see a sign: WELCOME HOME DAVE. And I knew that I must do it again.

Appendix 1

ZANE SPRAY

BRUCE ROBERTS'S SPRAY built in steel. 36 foot length, 12 foot beam, 4 foot draft.

DECK LAYOUT. Large raised poop deck, centre cockpit, raised pilot house with side windows, fore-cabin coach roof with mast tabernacle in front of pilot-house windscreen, narrow side decks with lowered working foredeck, $\frac{3}{4}$ inch and $\frac{1}{2}$ inch tube safety rails around all decks.

RIG. Cutter with both headsails furling. At start of voyage, main furling behind the mast, after Cape Town, three point slab reefing with all lines leading to the cockpit. Wooden mast 44 feet 6 inches high with single spreaders. Norsmen coated galvanized 8 mm wire for double backstays, fore-stays, jumper stays, lower and capping shrouds all with galvanized bottle-screws.

AFT-CABIN. One double berth with lockers underneath, steps to aft hatch and cockpit, passage through portside coaming by left of engine to pilot house. PILOT HOUSE. One single berth, chart table and access to large sail-locker in coaming on the starboard side, central steps down into fore-cabin under mast step, portside corner seat, at back of pilot house central aft steps to main hatch and cockpit. FORE-CABIN, heads to portside, galley to starboard, centre table with U-shaped seat, fore-hatch above, single berths port and starboard, forward anchor locker.

ENGINE. Massey Ferguson 165 (Perkins 203) marinized, offset from shaft, five V-belt drive with two-to-one reduction driving a $1\frac{1}{4}$ inch hollow shaft to a three-bladed 22 inch fully feathering variable pitch propeller, pitch control via gear boxes from cockpit to Renault car jack to push/pull rod down the centre of the shaft.

WHEEL STEERING. Via push/pull cables from cockpit to quadrant in the aft-cabin. SELF-STEERING by Sailomat bolted to the transom with controls to the cockpit.

WINCHES. At a cost of £30 each. Four out of six survived for 35,000 miles.

Appendix 2

1 140 amp arc welder, mains 230 volt.
5 boxes of welding rods.
1 Auto Arc DC welder working from engine.
1 set of sockets and spanners.
1 set of BA and Whitworth taps and dies.
36 drill bits.
2 electric drills.
1 electric router.
1 electric plane.
1 electric sander.
1 electric angle grinder.
1 electric jig saw.
2 hacksaws.
1 set wood chisels.
2 wood planes.
3 hammers.
1 mallet.
1 vice.
2 soldering irons.
1 locker with assorted electrical fittings, connectors,
   wire etc.
1 bolt cutter.
1 24 inch stillsons.
3 adjustable spanners.
1 4 lb club hammer.
4 cold chisels.

5 metal files.
2 hydrometers.
1 oil can.
2 pairs pliers.
2 pairs side cuts.
2 pairs bullnose pliers.
4 screwdrivers.
1 brace and assorted bits.
2 Stanley knives.
1 crowbar.
1 gas blow-lamp.

Appendix 3

BOAT'S STORES

1 gallon resin.
4 square yards fibreglass mat.
$\frac{1}{2}$ pint epoxy glue.
2 litres wood glue.
4 boxes of wood screws.
2 tubes super glue.
4 paint brushes.
2 paint rollers.
2 gas lamps.
2 hurricane lamps.
2 gallons paraffin.
4 spare wicks.
6 gallons two stroke petrol.
4 dozen assorted batteries.
4 bottles of CO_2 gas.
2 gallons anti-fouling paint.
6 gallons of assorted paints.
5 gallons waterproof grease.
1 pint rust converter.
4 boxes of assorted nuts and bolts.
2 gallons of engine oil.
3 cans WD40.
1 roll of sailcloth.
1 electric zig-zag sewing machine.
6 sail needles.
6 rolls of sail twine.
2 sailmaker's palms.

2 packets of bin liners.
6 large boxes of matches.
2 dozen distress flares.
1 Avon dinghy.
1 outboard motor, 4 hp.
2 Bruce anchors, 150 foot of chain.
1 box of 12 volt light bulbs.
3 dozen assorted shackles.
3 plastic buckets.
1 pack of Sailomat spares.
2 sets spare transmission belts.
1 spare water pump.
2 spare dry-charged 12 volt engine batteries.
1 typewriter.
6 club burgees.
1 Welsh dragon.
1 red ensign.
1 box of fish hooks and line.
1 spear gun.
1 shotgun with 36 cartridges.
6 tin openers.
6 large fenders.
500 foot of mooring ropes and spare sheets.

Appendix 4

3 dozen tins sardines.
2 dozen tins kippers.
2 dozen tins tuna.
2 dozen tins pilchards.
3 dozen tins minced beef.
3 dozen tins Irish stew.
2 dozen tins beef pie-filling.
2 dozen tins meat pies.
3 dozen assorted boxed meals.
3 dozen tins corned beef.
1 dozen tins luncheon meat.
3 dozen tins chunky chicken.
2 dozen meat and fish spreads.
2 dozen tins peas.
2 dozen tins green beans.
2 dozen tins broad beans.
3 dozen tins tomatoes.
3 dozen tins carrots.
2 dozen tins baked beans.
2 dozen packets Surprise peas.
2 dozen packets dried beans.
2 dozen tins fruit cocktail.
1 dozen tins Ideal Milk.
5 lbs dried milk.
2 dozen steamed fruit puddings.
2 tinned Guinness cakes.
1 dozen tins paté.

199

2 dozen tubes cheese and assorted spreads.
5 dozen packet soups.
5 dozen cup soups.
1 dozen packets assorted sauces.
6 bottles tomato sauce.
6 bottles brown sauce.
2 dozen packets yeast.
4 dozen packets Smash.
2 dozen tins of coleslaw.
4 dozen packets quick noodles.
6 lbs spaghetti.
4 lbs instant coffee.
2 lbs ground coffee.
2 lbs tea bags.
6 jars Marmite.
6 jars of assorted jam.
1 lb salt.
2 dozen packets salted peanuts.
6 pots black pepper.
56 lbs white flour.
10 lbs sugar.
10 lbs white rice.
20 sliced toasted loaves.
10 packets boiled sweets.
1 dozen tubs of margarine.
5 lbs dried fruit.
2 gallons of fruit squash.
2 dozen packets of assorted biscuits.
6 bottles each of Scotch, gin and rum.
4 dozen cans beer.
56 lbs potatoes.
20 lbs onions.
10 heads garlic.
5 lbs carrots.
5 lbs oranges.
2 large hard cabbages.
2 lbs popcorn.
4 dozen greased eggs.
4 packets vacuum packed bacon.
12 packets vacuum packed cheese.
5 litres cooking oil.
1 litre olive oil.

4 packets Rambout coffee filters.
12 small salamis.

12 tubes toothpaste.
48 rolls lavatory paper.
12 kitchen rolls.

Appendix 5

1 Yaesu 707 HAM radio.
1 Yaesu 700 antenna tuner.
1 G Whip 3 band antenna.
1 G5RV wire antenna.
1 VHF masthead antenna.
1 hand-held VHF antenna.
1 VHF 12 channel marine radio.
1 short wave radio cassette player.
1 Sony Walkman.
1 car radio.
1 short wave receiver kit.
1 Walker 412 satellite navigator.
1 sea spot radio direction finder.
1 Davis Mk 2 plastic sextant.
1 Plastimo log and depth finder.
1 Sestral fluxgate compass and relay.
1 hand-held compass.
1 Autohelm 3000 for wheel self-steering.
1 Sailomat for wind self steering.
1 radar alarm.

Appendix 6

3 dozen Disprin.
2 bottles Codeine.
1 bottle distalgesic.
6 courses of antibiotic.
3 packets sutures.
4 dozen dressings and bandages.
3 boxes Elastoplast.
1 packet Fisherman's Friends.
1 bottle strong pain killers.
3 bottles cough mixture.
6 common cold treatments.
1 large jar petroleum jelly.
1 inflatable splint.
3 slings.
1 box safety pins.
6 boxes anti-seasickness pills.
4 tubes burn cream.
6 bottles assorted vitamins.

Appendix 7

Ocean Passages Of The World.
Reed's Almanac.
1986 to 1988 *Nautical Almanac.*
The British Isles Pilot.
The Portuguese Pilot.
The African Pilots 1, 2 and 3.
The Australian Pilots, west, south and east.
The South American Pilots.
All charts to cover my route.
Norries' Tables.
The Lists of Lights A, D, K, G.
Photocopies and drawings of other charts.
Photocopies of sun sight forms.

ON BOARD CAMERAS

1 Bolex 16 mm film camera.
1 35 mm Richo still camera.
1 Sony 8 mm AM video camera.

Index

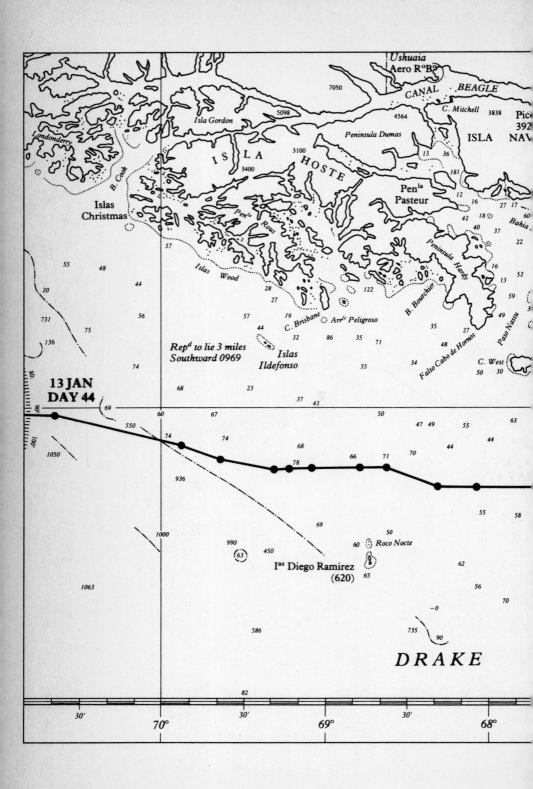

Ushuaia
Aero R°B°

CANAL BEAGLE
7050
C. Mitchell 3838
5098 Pic
4564 392
Peninsula Dumas ISLA
Isla Gordon NAV
I S L A 3100 HOSTE 13 36
3400 181
Pen^la
Islas Pasteur 12
Christmas 16 27 17
Pen^la 60
Rous 42 18 Bahia
57 40 37 22
55 48 Pen^la Rous 16
20 44 Islas Wood 13 52
56 28 57 59
731 27 B. Bourchier 35 49
75 19 C. Brisbane Arr^fe Peligroso 27
136 44 32 86 35 71 48 C. West
74 Rep^d to lie 3 miles Islas 55 34 50 30
Southward 0969 Ildefonso Falso Cabo de Hornos Paso Nassu
68 23
37 43
13 JAN 69 60 67 50 47 49 55 63
DAY 44 550 74 74 44 44
1050 936 68 66 71 70 44
69 78 50
1000 990 450 60 Roco Nocte 55 58
63 I^as Diego Ramirez 65 62
1063 (620) 56 70
586 735 90 −0
82
D R A K E

30' 70° 30' 69° 30' 68°